Praise for *The ...*

"Jeffrey Marx captures a remarkable story, and reveals a very human athlete with faith, doubt, and an underappreciated skill. *The Long Snapper* would be marvelous fiction; that this account is the ultimate truth is its great joy."

— Bob Ley, ESPN

"Jeffrey Marx has done it again, only better than ever. The improbable story of Brian Kinchen blooms in Marx's gifted hands. Thoughtful and inspiring, *The Long Snapper* is a quite simply a joy to behold."

— Rick Telander, *Chicago Sun Times*

"A great story."

— Vinny Testaverde

"Marx is a Pulitzer Prize–winning investigative journalist, and it shows in his vivid recreation of events long after the fact. That, in tandem with his ability to connect with Kinchen on a very human level, allows him to show a side of professional athletes rarely seen on Sunday broadcasts. It's an inspiring read for anyone who has ever wanted one last shot at their utmost dreams."

— *Publishers Weekly*

"A real-life inspirational story of a young man. . . . Kinchen's unexpected opportunity was wonderful on its own but more so because it clarified what was truly valuable in his life: marriage, family, and teaching. Nicely done, with plenty of insider football action."

— *Booklist*

THE LONG SNAPPER

Also by Jeffrey Marx

Season of Life

It Gets Dark Sometimes

One More Victory Lap (with Carl Lewis)

Inside Track (with Carl Lewis)

THE LONG SNAPPER

A Second Chance,
a Super Bowl,
a Lesson for Life

JEFFREY MARX

HarperOne
An Imprint of HarperCollinsPublishers

HarperOne

The poem "Focus" by Gus Kinchen on p. 66 and the unnamed poem by Trey Junkin on p. 160 are included by permission of the authors.

HarperCollins books may be purchased for educational, business, or sales promo-
tional use. For information please write: Special Markets Department, HarperCollins Publishers, 10 East 53rd Street, New York, NY 10022.

HarperCollins website: http://www.harpercollins.com
HarperCollins®, ■®, and HarperOne™ are
trademarks of HarperCollins Publishers.

FIRST HARPERCOLLINS PAPERBACK EDITION PUBLISHED IN 2011

Library of Congress Cataloging-in-Publication Data is available upon request.

ISBN 978–0–06–169138–6

11 12 13 14 15 RRD(H) 10 9 8 7 6 5 4 3 2 1

For Leslie Marx ("Po" to me)

This book is also dedicated to the memory of Wendy Marx,
my only sister and best friend,
and to all who save lives through organ donation and transplantation

Prologue

The job is probably the most obscure—and certainly the most unusual—in any of the major professional sports. It requires a big, strong man to submit to a stance that is both awkward and precarious. He is bent forward at the waist, legs apart, arms outstretched. His head is dropped and facing back between his legs. Looking upside down at the world, he grips a prolate spheroid, basically an oblong shape with pointed ends, covered with pebbled leather and adorned with eight white laces. Most people just call it a football. And the man now holding it, soon to be unleashing the ball on its way to being kicked by another player, is called the long snapper. As soon as he lets loose of the football, he will get clobbered and stepped on and generally abused—all well within the accepted rules of engagement in the National Football League.

The NFL employs thirty-two long snappers at a time—one per team in a limited but vital capacity that represents the evolution of sports into the era of specialized roles. If the long snapper does his job well, he will routinely perform before millions of people without ever being noticed. Total anonymity is considered perfection. And perfection is quite rewarding. In 2003, when our story begins, the average NFL long snapper was paid an annual salary of more than half a million dollars. He also ate and traveled extremely well—all courtesy of his employer—and the standard pampering and perks certainly did not stop there.

But this exalted existence at the highest level of sport can be transformed into sheer agony with such dizzying dispatch. A single mistake at the wrong time, just one little slip or lack of concentration at a critical moment in a big game, and if you are the long snapper, you're instant fodder for the media machine that never rests. You're on the evening news, the goat of your city. Your mistake is shown on ESPN over and over again, dissected in slow motion. You're an easy target on sports radio. And that's not even the worst of it. You could also be cut from the team. Fired.

There is always someone on the outside who desperately wants your job. He and his agent are constantly watching and waiting—watching for the first time a long snapper botches a play that costs his team a game, waiting for that perfect moment to call the general manager and encourage him to make a change.

You can also lose your cherished job through no fault of your own. Football being football, the most violent of American games, your season or even your entire career might just come to a halt by way of injury. Nothing you can do about that. Of course, given the zero-sum nature of professional sports, a dream denied for one automatically means the chance of a lifetime for another.

Nobody knew that better than Brian Kinchen.

One

He never really liked the idea of keeping his cell phone on while teaching. He certainly would not tolerate such behavior from the seventh graders in his Bible class at Parkview Baptist Middle School, especially not now, while reviewing for the end-of-semester final exam that was only two days away. But Brian Kinchen had a wife and four young sons. He could not imagine being unreachable in an emergency. The phone was tucked away, on silent, in the front left pocket of his slacks, when he felt it vibrate at 9:20 that Monday morning. The little screen showed an unfamiliar out-of-state number.

"Hello?"

"Hey, Brian, it's Scott Pioli."

An old friend from a previous existence.

Brian was an ex-jock. At the age of thirty-eight, after thirteen years of professional football and almost three years of searching for whatever might be next, he was new to teaching. He and Pioli were friends from their long-ago days together with the Cleveland Browns—Brian when he was a young player doing everything he could to keep his spot on the roster, Pioli when he was a young personnel assistant trying to move his way up in the front office. Pioli still worked in the NFL but now operated on a whole different level. As vice president of player personnel for the New England Patriots, he was one of the most respected executives in the league, working closely with head coach Bill Belichick, who was on his way to becoming the NFL's winningest coach of the decade. Together they had orchestrated the franchise's first Super Bowl victory after the 2001 season. And now—with only two weeks left in the 2003 regular season—the Patriots were well positioned for another championship run.

Brian and Pioli had not spoken for nearly a year. *Why this out-of-nowhere call at a time when his schedule has to be crazy?* Brian wondered. *Must be about that hat I asked him to have Belichick sign for that lady I met.* After the obligatory small talk, Brian cut to the chase: "Hey, man, where's my hat? I never got the hat."

Pioli had an entirely different agenda.

"Listen," he said. "You're not gonna believe this, Brian, but we need to get a look at you. Bill wants to get a look at you."

Brian was familiar enough with football-speak to know exactly what that meant. His old coach—Belichick had been head coach in Cleveland when Brian and Pioli were there—wanted to fly him into Boston for a tryout. Brian was absolutely stunned. He paced in front of his class.

"You're serious?"

"Our long snapper got hurt," Pioli said.

Most of the two dozen students were distracted from working on their review material, trying to figure out what in the world their teacher was dealing with on the phone.

"I'm thirty-eight years old," Brian said.

Pioli already knew that, of course, but Brian was only thinking out loud. "You realize how long it's been since I've played football? I mean, I still work out, just went to the gym before school this morning, but I'm probably down about twenty pounds from the end of my career."

Brian stood almost six-foot-three and now weighed less than 220, big for everyday life, but not for someone banging heads with defensive linemen in the NFL.

"Not a problem," Pioli said. "We just need you to snap. We don't need you to block. Don't need you to cover. Just snap. Just get the ball back there."

"Really?"

"Wouldn't be calling if I didn't mean it."

Brian was excited but also wary. Those painful memories he'd been trying to push away—the indignity of rejection and the empty feeling of worthlessness—came rushing back, once again washing all over him. What to do? What to tell his friend?

"I really don't know if I want to do this," Brian said. "I'll have to think about it. Can you give me a couple hours?"

"I'll call you back," Pioli said.

The teacher turned to his curious students and took in a deep breath. Gathering himself as best he could, Brian said, "You guys are not gonna believe who that was. This guy from the New England Patriots, Scott Pioli, he wants me to fly up there and try to make the team. He wants me to play football again."

It is not often that a Bible class turns into a free-for-all. Students shouted and cheered, so many voices competing for attention that Brian could not immediately make out the particulars of what anyone was saying. All that registered was the overall excitement emanating even from those who did not have a clue about football. But then came a voice of clarity through the cacophony. It belonged to a boy in the back of the classroom: "The Patriots have the best record in the league. Everyone's picking them to win it all this year." That was an overstatement; not everyone was picking the Patriots. But New England was indeed projected to be one of the strong favorites heading into the playoffs. The Patriots had won twelve of fourteen games—including their last ten in a row—and were tied with the Kansas City Chiefs for the best record in the NFL. Brian had no idea about any of that. He had not been paying much attention to professional football. Turning his back on the game he loved was the only way he could deal with its having unceremoniously dumped him after all those years.

"What do y'all think?" Brian asked.

"Awesome," one of the girls shouted.

"You gotta go," one of the boys said.

Then came a chorus of concurrence.

"Yeah, go, Mr. Kinchen."

"You have to. You have to."

Brian settled everyone down and shared an idea. He would take a vote: "Raise your hand if you think I should go." There was no need to count. Every student—boys and girls—had at least one hand up. Some were enthusiastically stabbing the air with both hands. The vote was unanimous. And the students erupted again.

"We'll watch you on TV," one of the boys blurted out. "How cool is that?"

If only it were that simple for Brian. Of course, none of the kids knew about the ugly ending and the string of rejections he had already endured. Brian had not only been a long snapper in the NFL. He had been a decent tight end as well, gaining recognition primarily for his blocking and tenacity, but also catching as many as fifty-five passes in a single season, 1996, while playing for the Baltimore Ravens. The apparent end to his playing career came four years later with the Carolina Panthers, after a knee injury and months of clinging to the false hope that his job would still be there for him the next year. Instead, after surgery and rehabilitation, Brian was cut loose. For a while, he remained optimistic about catching on with another team. But nobody called. Brian was crushed.

Professional athletes almost uniformly voice the desire to retire "on their own terms," a vague and shifting goal that is rarely realized. And they are often filled with regret and separation anxiety when closure does not come so neatly wrapped. Brian was by no means the first to struggle upon departure from the high-profile world of professional sports. Back in his hometown of Baton Rouge, where he had attended Louisiana State University (LSU), he certainly enjoyed the extra time with his family and the practically endless freedom to play golf. But Brian missed the intensity of the NFL and the camaraderie of teammates. He missed having a schedule and a specific purpose every day. He became depressed. And that was before the onslaught of disappointments.

His second year out of football, 2002, Brian decided that he would no longer sit around waiting for someone to invite him back into the NFL. He would start calling people himself. So what if his thirty-seventh birthday would arrive before the start of the season? Surely someone could use a long snapper who had been steady and dependable for thirteen years as a professional. So he started reaching out to people he knew.

The first thread of hope was extended by a former college teammate who was now working in player personnel for the Dallas Cowboys. Toward the end of summer training camp, right after their long snapper had struggled in a pre-season game, the Cowboys invited Brian in for a tryout. He thought he snapped as well as he ever had. The *Dallas Morning News* even reported that the Cowboys were expected to sign him. But they decided to go with a younger player, and Brian was sent home without so much as a hello or good-bye from head coach Dave Campo.

A few weeks later, Brian got another shot, this time with the Pittsburgh Steelers. Their long snapper, Mike Schneck, was expected to miss six weeks with a dislocated elbow, and their special-teams coach, Kevin Spencer, had started his NFL coaching career in Cleveland while Brian was playing with the Browns. Brian's confidence was further bolstered by the fact that he'd played for three other Pittsburgh assistants either in college or in the NFL. That only made the outcome all the more frustrating. After throwing what he considered perfect strikes in his tryout and thinking the job was his, Brian was offered nothing but a ride back to the airport. Once again, he had not even been allowed an audience with the head coach. Having been told that Bill Cowher was "in meetings" and too busy to see him, Brian seethed the whole way home. After all those years in the NFL, he thought that he should be treated with at least some degree of respect. He was devastated by the Pittsburgh trip.

One more blow was yet to come. Midway through the 2002 season, the Denver Broncos were looking strong after winning six of eight games. Less than thrilled with the play of his kicking teams, however, head coach Mike Shanahan wanted to make a few changes. He was in the market for a new long snapper. Brian knew Shanahan and again thought he had a reasonable chance of being signed. He was invited to Denver for a tryout. He felt that his snaps were flawless. Then—without explanation and without ever seeing Shanahan—he was again passed over for a younger guy. Was it simply a matter of opting for youth? Was Brian considered too risky because of his less-than-perfect knee? Did league salary rules—his thirteen years of NFL service dictating that he'd have to be paid considerably more than a newcomer—have anything to do with it?

"I don't know what the deal is," Brian told his wife, Lori, on the phone. "But I'm not putting myself through this anymore. Too much of an emotional roller coaster. I'm done."

It was not until the flight home that both the reality and the finality of that really hit him. His dejection stemmed not only from the worthlessness he felt after going zero-for-three in tryouts or from the absolute belief that he was unmistakably done this time. No, Brian struggled with something much bigger and broader and more debilitating than that—a blindness. It was simply impossible to see himself the way almost anyone else would view him: as a highly successful athlete who had parlayed his Hercules-like build and considerable abilities into a remarkably long (for football) and prosperous career. It was impossible because—after all the dreaming and the training and the stretching of limits and the sacrifices—Brian could see only one word hanging over the entirety of his efforts: *failure*. All he'd ever wanted was to establish himself as an impact player, someone who would long be remembered and who might even accomplish something worthy of mention in the football history books. The mere thought of that desire now brought such discomfort and sorrow. Brian had a beautiful wife and four healthy children waiting for him at home. He had a profound spiritual grounding that had guided him and served him well for as long as he could remember. Yet there was nothing he could do on that plane to shake that one word—*failure, failure, failure*—and the depth of hurt that it triggered.

The thoughts kept taunting him: *I was just another guy who wore a jersey. Nothing really spectacular ever happened in my career. All I ever did was try to legitimize myself. But now I'll never get what I've always wanted, what I've always* needed. *I'll never have that stamp of approval that I really made it. No validation. No finality on my own terms.*

Speaking for the broad universe of professional athletes, Hall of Fame quarterback Steve Young describes retirement from the NFL as the emotional equivalent of falling off a cliff. "You're at the top of your field, and then suddenly you're done," he says. "I was great at football, but I haven't been that great at anything since. And once that sinks in, that realization is really hard."

Brian had done the best he could to pack away the emotional residue left from his fall off the cliff. And teaching seemed to be the right "next thing" for him. He truly felt he was employing his talents exactly as God intended. And he had even found several avocations—coaching middle school football at Parkview, helping the LSU football staff as a volunteer assistant, playing celebrity golf tournaments all over the country—that again allowed him to enjoy all that was good in sports. Now, though, he was flooded with confusion and doubt. Sure, he felt a lift from the blind affirmation enthusiastically offered by his students when he explained the phone call from the Patriots. He also felt a jolt of hope that perhaps there was still something left of his football career, maybe even the defining moment that had always somehow eluded him. But then there was the dread: *What if I'm just being set up for yet another letdown? If I really found what I'm supposed to be doing, teaching, then how can I justify just picking up and taking off from school simply because some football team needs a long snapper, just because* I *might deep inside be starving for one final shot at the NFL?*

His students would have been stunned had they known the turmoil that churned inside of him. After all, he was always big, strong, confident Mr. Kinchen to them, Coach Kinchen to some, a former professional athlete whose exterior walls were built with layer upon layer of absolute certainty. The boys who were into sports thought he was just about the coolest guy they'd ever known. The girls focused on his rugged good looks—the overall build, the chiseled face with pronounced chin and well-defined jaw lines, the hazel eyes and thick brown hair, the radiant smile. But physical shell and emotional facade meant nothing now. Brian felt extremely vulnerable.

He called his wife, who was only a building away. Lori often worked as a substitute teacher at Parkview and had also been coaching fifth- and sixth-grade cheerleading. She happened to be teaching that morning in the elementary school.

"You'll never guess who called me," Brian said.

"Who?"

"Scott Pioli. They want me to go to New England."

"To coach?" Lori said.

"No, to *play.*"

"Shut up, Brian. There's no way."

He offered details and convinced her that he was telling the truth. Then the conversation turned to making a decision. Brian explained that Pioli would be calling back shortly and wanted him at the airport as soon as possible.

"I really don't think I want to go," Brian told his wife. "I just don't want to deal with the rejection again."

"Well, what about living the rest of your life wondering what might have happened?" Lori replied. "I mean, let's say you go and then they don't sign you. At least you tried. It's a lot easier to live with something you at least tried than to live with the regret that you didn't even give it a chance. If you don't go, you'll have to live with that regret your whole life."

"True. I guess I need to think about that."

"The worst thing that happens is you're gone for a couple days. Maybe they'll let me take your classes for you. I already know most of the kids. It wouldn't be that big a deal."

"No."

"And then if the Patriots end up signing you and you're up there for a while, with Christmas break coming, you wouldn't even be missing that much school."

Brian paused. Then he said, "Let's talk again in a little while. I want to go get a football and see what it feels like."

By this point, the students had a pretty good feel for their first-year teacher. They knew that Brian was unmistakably serious when it came to the understanding of Bible stories and concepts, but they also appreciated that he consistently tried to foster a fairly light atmosphere in the classroom. The first day of school he had been asked by one of the students what they were supposed to call him. This was a somewhat confusing matter because many of the kids had already known him before he started teaching. He had coached some of the boys in football. His wife had coached some of the girls in cheerleading. And some of the kids had long been friends with his two oldest sons: Austin was now in eighth grade, and Hunter was in sixth. "Okay, we have a few choices," Brian told his first class. "You can call me Mr. Kinchen, Mr. Brian, Coach Kinchen . . . or Professor." Everyone laughed. "Yeah, I like the sound of that," Brian said, with mock seriousness. "*Professor.* Really stuffy, formal guy. That's me." It was so *not* him that some of the students got a kick out of calling him that and still did sometimes.

Even knowing Brian the way they did, they were still surprised when he announced that they were taking a break from reviewing for the final exam. He was going to get a football from the athletic department, and they were all going outside so he could show them what a long snapper does. Actually, Brian also had another reason—the one he'd shared with Lori—that he wanted to get his hands on a football. Before hearing back from Pioli, he wanted to be certain that he could still throw it between his legs with the same power and precision that had always come so easily to him. Brian had no reason to think it would be a problem, but he wanted to make sure. Fortunately, he was in a climate that would comfortably allow for a spontaneous class outing in the middle of December. The sky was clear, and the temperature was fifty-three degrees.

Brian led his students outside to an open stretch of grass, dirt, and gravel between their two-story brick school building and the collection of swings, slides, and climbing apparatus that filled the playground. He marked off fifteen yards and explained the measurement to those who didn't know what it represented: the distance a long snapper typically throws the football from the line of scrimmage—where a play begins—to a punter who will kick the ball away to the other team.

"Come catch some for me," Brian said to one of his students, Wesley Perkins, who was one of the better football players in the seventh grade.

Brian stretched his arms and shoulders. Standing upright, he threw a few passes—just as a quarterback would—to make sure he was loose. Then he tugged at his dress slacks for better mobility and bent forward toward the ground. He gripped the football with both hands and stared back through his legs at Wesley's outstretched hands.

"Ready?" Brian asked in an upside-down shout.

"Ready," Wesley said.

Brian fired away and . . . *thwack* . . . Wesley felt the hard leather and unforgiving laces of the football violate the soft skin of his palms.

"Wow," Wesley said.

The other students oohed and aahed. None of them had any idea that the ball would be zipping so fast through the air. The average

NFL snapper requires between seven- and eight-tenths of a second to cover the fifteen yards from his grip to the hands of a punter.

"How was the spiral?" Brian wanted to know.

"Perfect," Wesley said.

"Let's do it again."

Wesley caught close to a dozen snaps.

"Where was it?" Brian asked after each.

"Right down the middle," Wesley kept reporting. Only once did a snap move slightly off center. But then the next one was right on target again.

"Spiral was good?" Brian said.

"Better than my passes!" Wesley answered.

Other students stepped in to try catching a snap or two. A couple of the boys were able to hold on. None of the girls had much success, usually just knocking the ball down or even jumping out of the way before it reached them, but they had no problem screaming and laughing and playfully wrapping themselves in the excitement of it all. After a while, four girls decided that they would stand together—one big target—and that one of them would somehow come up with a catch. "We're getting it this time," Ashley Thornton said. But when Brian let loose of the football, one of the other girls simply swatted it to the ground and they all went right back to giggling.

Brian still had work to do. He cut the distance almost in half, marking a spot about seven and three-quarters yards away, right where he would want a holder positioned to catch and place the ball for a kicker to attempt a field goal or an extra point after a touchdown. Wesley got down on a knee and held out a hand for Brian to target.

Thwack. Thwack. Thwack.

With a shorter distance to travel, the ball was coming in even harder now. Lower and harder. Right on target.

Pretty amazing, Wesley thought. *Does he ever miss?*

When the bell rang to signal the end of class, Brian's students returned to the normal flow of their school day, gathering up books and knapsacks, scurrying off to their next classes. Brian stayed behind for a few moments, staring at the ground, pondering his predicament: *I want to submit to God's plan, but what is it? I thought I was supposed to be here at the school, and I made a commitment to teaching. But now am I supposed to go?* Brian silently asked for help: *Please, Lord, give me some kind of clarity.*

Brian soon found that clarity in the form of encouragement from others. He spoke to his dad on the telephone. He called an old LSU teammate—Tommy Hodson, one of his best friends from college—who had gone on to play quarterback for the Patriots in the early 1990s. He visited with the school principal, Cooper Pope. Their responses were all similar: "What a great opportunity. What are you even thinking about?" When Brian explained to Pope that he was struggling with the thought of breaking his commitment to the school, the principal encouraged him not to look at it that way. "It's a no-brainer," Pope said. "This is something you need to do. You gotta go play if you can. And, no matter what happens, the experience will serve the school and the kids well. This might be a God-created opportunity for you to go do something and then bring it back to share with the kids." That made Brian feel better. By the time he was done processing, he was certain he had to go for the tryout. He was also sorry he had ever asked Pioli for time to think about it: *What if he's already found someone else while he's waiting to call me back?*

Brian had two more classes before lunch. He opened each with an explanation of what was happening with the Patriots. Then he did the best he could to concentrate on reviewing. Really, though, all he was doing was waiting for his cell phone to ring. When it finally did, he was relieved to see Pioli's number on the screen.

Brian had a question for him: "Is there any way you can guarantee that I'm actually gonna get the job?"

"Can't promise you anything," Pioli said. "You know how it works."

"Yeah, I understand," Brian said. "But you can at least promise me I'm gonna see Belichick, right? I mean, if I'm going all the way up there, I am *not* leaving without at least a 'hello' from the guy."

After those three painful tryouts the year before, three straight rejections without even seeing the head coaches, Brian was doing emotional damage control.

"Not a problem," Pioli said. "You'll definitely see Bill. You have my word on that."

"Good," Brian said. "So what do I need to do?"

Pioli put an assistant on the line to discuss travel plans. Only a few days after sitting at a computer and putting together the final exam for his seventh-grade Bible students, formulating questions about miracles and morality and free will, Brian now had all of about three hours before he had to be at the airport.

After making final arrangements with school administrators—Lori would indeed handle his classes while he was gone—Brian went home for toiletries and a change of clothes. That was it: just one day's worth of essentials. If he ended up signing with the

Patriots, Lori would ship more clothes to him. But there was no reason to get ahead of himself. He and his family had been around football plenty long enough—three generations' worth of blocking and tackling and life-changing drama—to know that virtually anything could happen.

Two

Jacob Calvin Kinchen had a lot to consider when it came time, on June 7, 1938, to name his first child, starting with the fact that he had never really liked his own first name. That was why he called himself Jake and those closest to him just used the initials J.C. Perhaps that would have been enough to push any less of a football man toward the choice of a safe name that would always be comfortable for his child. But Jake could not help himself. He had been captain of his high school football team, the Albany Panthers, 1934 district champions in Livingston Parish, Louisiana, and he had become a coach at nearby Live Oak High School. How serious was Jake Kinchen about training his players? "He would get us in front of his car in this little lane that was fenced in, and then he would start driving," one of his first student-athletes, Odom Graves, would still vividly remember some seventy years later. "You didn't have any choice but to run." Only a man with such passion for sport could possibly look beyond his own discomfort with the seemingly benign name of Jacob and name his son . . . Gaynell.

Brian Kinchen's father was named after one of the era's most famous people in Louisiana: Gaynell Tinsley, the first All-American football player at LSU. Tinsley was a unanimous pick for the Associated Press team in both 1935 and 1936. He went on to play professionally for the Chicago Cardinals, and in his rookie year of 1937 he led the NFL in receiving yardage. During the off-season that followed, his given name was introduced to the Kinchen family tree.

Naturally, Gaynell Kinchen started playing football when he was quite young. He loved the game, but he despised the childhood razzing that came with such an unusual name. Much to Gaynell's relief, he was eventually bailed out by a coach during his freshman year at Baton Rouge High School. The coach started calling him "Gus" because that was Gaynell Tinsley's nickname. "Gus" Kinchen would have been plenty happy if his link to the former LSU star had ended there. It did not. Their shared name was only the beginning. Before long, Gus Kinchen would himself become something of a folkloric figure in the rich history of LSU football.

Nothing about his first two collegiate seasons foretold anything but frustration. Playing on the 1956 freshman team, Kinchen severely injured his left knee, which had already required surgery in high school, and he underwent another operation. Still unable to play as a sophomore, he served in the menial role of team manager, hauling equipment and running errands for the coaches.

These were also humbling times for the LSU football program as a whole. In 1955, LSU had hired a new coach, thirty-year-old Paul

Dietzel, who arrived in Baton Rouge as the youngest head coach in major college football. He had a sign painted for the entrance to the LSU practice field, optimistically welcoming his charges to "The Proving Grounds." But after winning only eleven of thirty games in three years under Dietzel, the LSU Tigers had proved only their own mediocrity. More of the same was predicted for 1958. A preseason poll of sportswriters placed LSU eighth in the twelve-team Southeastern Conference. Tiger Stadium held 67,510 seats, but expectations were so low that tickets were printed for only 30,000 of them. There were grumblings that Dietzel had to go.

Then magic happened.

The turning point was Dietzel's decision to break his squad into three permanent units and play an unusual style of platoon football. The eleven best players would play about the first half of each quarter on both offense and defense. Two backup units, one on offense, the other on defense, would split the remaining playing time. This would allow the best players to stay fresher. It would also boost team morale, because more players would actually get to play.

The new system brought immediate success. Winning game after game was itself quite a surprise. But the most unexpected outcome was the stellar performance of the least talented of the three units: the defensive specialists, who came to be known as the Chinese Bandits. The name came from a popular comic strip, "Terry and the Pirates," in which artist Milton Caniff had characterized Chinese bandits as the meanest and most vicious people in the world. That was exactly what Dietzel wanted in his defensive unit. Gus Kinchen, still hampered by his bad knee but finally back on the field, played right end for the Bandits and quickly became a leader.

"Bless his heart, he didn't have any speed and he wasn't very big," teammate Don "Scooter" Purvis would later say. "But Gus was one of the best technique players you'd ever see. He had the savvy and the know-how. He was never out of position—always covering his assignment. And he was just an excellent leader. Gus didn't lead by shouting and hollering. He led by example. He was the type of person you wanted to emulate because of his dedication."

Three things happened as LSU continued winning: The Tigers kept climbing the national rankings. School officials scrambled to print more tickets. And the Chinese Bandits kept gaining popularity.

For the rest of his life, Dietzel would say without hesitation that he never had any thrill greater than coaching the Bandits. They were so enthusiastic, so wild, and they *hustled*. They taught him more about gang tackling than any team he had ever coached—or ever would.

Fans simply loved the Bandits—and the Chinese theme started popping up everywhere. Thousands of people wore straw coolie hats to the games. The LSU cheerleaders unfurled a large banner with "So Lau Yah" ("Hold That Line") written in Chinese characters. A Memphis disc jockey wrote a Chinese Bandit chant that the LSU band put to music and played in the stadium:

> *Chinese bandits on their way,*
> *Listen to what Confucius say.*
> *Chinese bandits, they can knock,*
> *Gonna stop a touchdown—chop-chop!*

Players on the other two units got plenty of attention, too, especially do-it-all halfback Billy Cannon, who would win the Heisman Trophy the next year. But the Bandits were often front and center when it came to fan frenzy and media coverage. Six games into the season and still undefeated, LSU was for the first time voted number one in the Associated Press college football poll. "They Did It!!" screamed the banner headline in the *Baton Rouge Morning Advocate* of October 28, 1958. Directly under the headline—looming large across six columns—was a graphic designed to look like the page of a Chinese newspaper but with posed action photos of Kinchen and fellow Bandit Merle Schexnaildre superimposed on it. *Sports Illustrated* and *Life* magazine would later run prominent feature stories on the Bandits—the former declaring them "the darlings of the South" and the latter including a large color photo of them wearing football uniforms and wicked-looking Chinese masks with yellow-green faces and black Fu Manchu mustaches. After the tenth and final regular-season game, in which LSU clobbered Tulane, 62–0, to remain undefeated and lock up the national championship (then decided before bowl games), AP writer W.B. Ragsdale Jr. said of the Bandits: "This is possibly the most publicized substitute team in college football history and probably the proudest."

In response to the perfect regular season, LSU rewarded Dietzel with a new five-year contract that would pay him $16,500 a year (a raise of $2,500). The same day that was reported in the local paper—in fact, directly under the Dietzel story that ran in the Sunday *Advocate* on December 7, 1958—another headline trumpeted more good news for the football program: "LSU Signs

Kinchen To Grant-in-Aid." Gary Kinchen, an All-State guard for Baton Rouge High School, was the first local signee of the year and would soon join big brother Gus in Tiger Stadium. Of course, neither of them gave any thought to how far the Kinchen football tradition might someday reach. They were just happy to be college teammates.

LSU went on to defeat Clemson, 7–0, in the Sugar Bowl. For the season, LSU had given up fewer than five points per game, outscoring its opponents by a stunning margin of 282 to 53. At the end of 1958, the Tigers were named AP "Team of the Year" not only for college football but for the whole of American sports, beating out the New York Yankees of Mickey Mantle and the Baltimore Colts of Johnny Unitas.

Gus Kinchen's popularity extended well beyond the football field. He was chosen to serve on the fashion panel of a downtown department store. He was invited to speak at church events and youth banquets. And he was later elected president of the LSU Student Government Association. It was in that role that Kinchen booked comedian Bob Hope to perform at LSU. Playing to a crowd of ten thousand that was well familiar with the Chinese Bandits, Hope had the theatrical flair to wear a coolie hat when he greeted Kinchen on stage. The place went wild.

Then there was the girl. As if life were not already grand enough for Kinchen, he also ended up with the campus beauty. His girlfriend, LSU cheerleader Toni Whittington, was voted "Darling of LSU" both her freshman and sophomore years. She was the reason a new rule was established to disallow repeat winners: the powers that be simply wanted to give someone else a chance. A local writer described Toni as "petite . . . with sparkling brown eyes and a pixie smile . . . a brunette with lustrous dark brown hair." On December 23, 1961, Gaynell "Gus" Kinchen and Maude Ann "Toni" Whittington were married in her hometown of Natchitoches, Louisiana.

Forty-two years later, heading into the Baton Rouge airport for his trip to Boston and his final shot at football, Brian Kinchen walked unmistakably alone. Nobody else entering the building could possibly have known what was stirring within him: the thought that one trip, one tryout, could be filled with such tremendous possibility. Maybe he could finally find the validation and accomplishment for which he had always striven. But Brian was not flying off just for himself. He was also flying off for Jake Kinchen and for Gus Kinchen and for anyone else—young or old, athlete or not—who would understand what it meant when a man needed to prove himself on a field of play.

Three

The first flight of the day—from Baton Rouge to Atlanta—was uneventful. But the connecting flight to Boston offered quite a surprise. During the boarding process, Brian Kinchen glanced up from his window seat and saw a familiar face passing by in the aisle. Their eyes locked for just a moment.

"Hey, Brian, what's going on?" Harper LeBel said.

"Hey, how are you?" Brian said.

With a stream of passengers bustling for position, LeBel kept moving without a chance for any real conversation. Brian initially thought it was bizarre to randomly run into someone he had not even thought about for years. But then he started connecting the dots: *Wait a minute. He's going to the same place I am . . . trying out for the same job!* LeBel was another out-of-work long snapper. He'd been out of the NFL even longer than Brian. In the world of football, he might as well have been Methuselah; LeBel was forty! What really jarred Brian was recalling the way LeBel's otherwise steady ten-year career had come to a nightmarish end in Baltimore. That was where they had gotten to know each other, as teammates with the Baltimore Ravens in 1998. After Brian tore a tendon in his right thumb during training camp, LeBel was given the opportunity to take his place until he healed. The results were disastrous. In the season opener, a 20–13 loss to the Pittsburgh Steelers, LeBel pretty much blew the game with three bad snaps—one that led directly to a Pittsburgh touchdown and two that caused his own kicker to miss field goals—thereby earning the honorific "Goat of the Week" from writer Peter King of *Sports Illustrated*. Four games later, LeBel had another major meltdown, with multiple poor snaps on punts. That was the end of professional football for him. Reflecting on that experience during the flight to Boston, Brian could not help but think: *Five years after that debacle, without ever playing again, and Harper LeBel is getting a tryout with the Patriots? How in the world does that happen?*

When they got off the plane, Brian and LeBel found each other in the terminal and walked together through Logan International Airport, catching up on what they'd been doing since their lives had last intersected in Baltimore. LeBel had not checked any luggage, either, so they went straight past the baggage carousels and outside to the curb, where someone from the Patriots was supposed to pick them up. They waited . . . and waited. And they shivered. The temperature was thirty degrees, fairly extreme for two guys just arriving from the South without sufficient outerwear, and with the wind whipping, they might as well have been stranded on an iceberg in the middle of nowhere.

Finally, a van pulled up for them. It was late because the driver had been waiting elsewhere at the airport for the two other men now introducing themselves to Brian and LeBel. They, too, were unemployed long snappers. One was Chance Pearce, just in from College Station, Texas, twenty-three and still seeking his first NFL job after having been drafted but later released by the Houston Texans before the start of the 2003 season. The other was Dan O'Leary, from the Cleveland area, twenty-six and already an NFL veteran, having played partial seasons in 2001 with the Buffalo Bills and in 2002 with the Pittsburgh Steelers and the New York Giants. Although Brian had never met O'Leary and had no idea who he was when they shook hands in the van, it was he who had gotten the temporary Pittsburgh job for which Brian had auditioned the previous year. There was one other link between the two men. Playing high school football in Cleveland while Brian was playing for the hometown Browns, O'Leary had always been a big fan of his because they both played tight end in addition to long snapping. *God, is this the same Brian Kinchen?* O'Leary now wondered. *Still out here after all these years?* As a teenager, he had always wanted to be like Brian—he had watched him so closely that he still remembered Brian's jersey number, eighty-eight, with the Browns—and now he was actually sitting right there with him. Even more amazing, he was on his way to compete against the guy for a job. *Unbelievable,* O'Leary thought.

And off they went—four men sharing both a ride and a dream. The van had ample space for all. The dream had room for only one.

During the season, Tuesday is generally the quietest day at the practice complex of an NFL team. Injured players visit the training room for treatment, and a few other guys might show up to lift weights or watch game film. For the most part, though, players are off, and this is the best time for all who work closest with them to dial down the intensity and take advantage of the respite to regroup for the next battle. Coaches work on game plans. Trainers restock supplies. Equipment managers repair helmets and shoulder pads. If the front office is looking to make a roster change, Tuesday is also the ideal day to conduct a player tryout. Track down and fly in a few free agents on Monday. Get them up early Tuesday for the team doctor to examine them. Have them on a practice field by mid-morning. And so it was for the four long snappers who were delivered by van to Gillette Stadium in Foxborough, Massachusetts, home of the Patriots, on the morning of Tuesday, December 16, 2003.

They dressed in a small locker room—the one used by referees on game days—in the bowels of the stadium. Then they went outside and got a ride across a large parking lot to the entrance of an indoor practice facility generally referred to as the "bubble." From the van to the door, the silence of stress was violated only by a single sound familiar to anyone who has ever been around football: the loud click-clacking of cleats striking concrete. The noise lessened and then stopped altogether as the long snappers filed inside—their cleats now quietly sinking with each step into the soft cushion of turf.

Brian gazed across the perfectly lined field. Walking slowly and taking in the sight of a few team officials with stopwatches and notepads at the ready, then noticing another staffer armed with video equipment, Brian could hardly believe he was once again subjecting himself to this glorified meat market known as a group tryout: *Can't believe I'm right back in the middle of this craziness. Can't believe how long it's been since I've even thought about all this stuff.*

Brian and the three other Patriot wannabes were greeted by special-teams coach Brad Seely, who asked them to pair up and get loose. Brian worked with Pearce, stretching and tossing a ball back and forth, while LeBel and O'Leary did the same. After a few minutes, Seely said that they would begin the tryout with punt snaps, still working in pairs. O'Leary lined up to go first, with LeBel fifteen yards behind him to catch his snaps. Alongside O'Leary, separated by a couple of yards, stood Pearce, who would snap to Brian. Of course, each snapper would be concentrating not only on his own work; though wanting to be subtle about it, he would also be checking out how the others performed. In the early going, with O'Leary and Pearce alternating snaps, Brian did not see anything that really impressed him. *Pretty average,* he thought. Then came the first ugly mishap of the day: Pearce threw a wild ball over Brian's head and beyond his reach. As the football bounced and then skidded away, so too did any real possibility that the young man from Texas might be getting a job that day. *He's done,* Brian told himself. *Three of us left.*

Once O'Leary and Pearce had each made about a dozen snaps, they swapped spots with LeBel and Brian. LeBel's first snap was high but catchable, nothing that would cost him too much even in the unforgiving evaluation now taking place. Still, he was upset that he started that way. He looked up at the ceiling and reminded himself of rule one: *Relax!* After that, LeBel felt that his snaps were "nails"—right where he wanted them. Brian's assessment was much more critical: *He's all over the place. Low. High. Nothing really bad. But pretty inconsistent.* LeBel and Brian did share a general overview on which they'd agreed since their time together in Baltimore: LeBel threw a harder ball, which was quite impressive when it ended up exactly where he wanted it, but Brian was more consistent with his spiral and placement.

Brian was pleased with his own performance in this first round of snapping in punt formation. Considering how long it had been since he had played football, Brian also felt surprisingly fluid and strong firing up into blocking position after letting loose of the ball. It was one of his assets that LeBel and many others in the NFL had long admired. Brian had spent years among the best at everything a snapper needs to do once the ball is released: popping up to block, quickly thrusting his arms forward into combat position; fighting off an enemy who is seeking instant gratification in the form of a blocked punt; and then charging downfield to cover the punt and maybe even make a tackle.

Next in the tryout came the shorter snaps—seven and a half to almost eight yards, depending on personal preference—to a holder who would rest one knee on the ground and simulate the position he'd be in to place the ball for the kicker on a field goal or extra point after a touchdown. With the distance greatly reduced (basically cut in half) from the snaps in punt formation, the likelihood of error was also significantly diminished. But the whole operation could still be altogether ruined with one simple slip or lapse in concentration.

Thinking only about mechanics and focusing on his target, Brian got off to a perfect start on his first few snaps at the shorter distance. Then came disaster. He sailed one right over the holder's head. Brian was shocked and had no idea how it happened. He had never before thrown one so high like that, not in his whole life— not in practice, not in a game. Low, yes. Off target to the right or to the left, yes. But never high enough to where the guy had to leave his knee and still couldn't get to it.

None of the other snappers said anything. But they all came to the same conclusion: *Kinchen's done. No way he gets the job after that fiasco.* Up to that point, it was hard for LeBel not to think that Brian was the favorite simply because he had played for Belichick in Cleveland. But now the door was open for the others. That was the one moment when LeBel had just a little smile on his face.

Brian was well aware that one errant snap was usually all it took to be eliminated during a group tryout. *I blew it,* he silently conceded. *I'm outta here.* But he also told himself: *Just keep on going. Maybe they'll screw up, too.* Wanting to put the bad snap behind him as quickly as possible, Brian grabbed another ball, positioned himself over it, and fired it back to the holder. *Thwack.* He was right on target this time. Brian moved off to the side, and the other snappers went through another rotation.

When everyone was done, Seely singled out Brian for some extra work: "Hey, Brian, let's get a few more short snaps before we go." Brian did not know what to think of that. Neither did the other guys. They just stood off to the side—everything was so entirely out of their control now—while Brian concluded the tryout with four additional snaps. They were all bull's-eyes. But the clean finish did nothing to lessen the overwhelming frustration of that one bad snap. A combination of disappointment and anger consumed Brian as he walked off the field, head hanging low. All he could think was: *I cannot believe I just blew that. Best opportunity I've ever had, with the best team in football, last opportunity I'll ever have . . . and I blow it like that.*

Back in the locker room, Brian went straight for his cell phone to give Lori the bad news. "I just can't believe I threw it over the guy's head," Brian said. "I've never done that. Never! I just can't believe it happens now. I don't know how they could possibly give me the job after that."

"Well, Belichick hasn't said anything yet, has he?" Lori said.

"No," Brian said. "I'll call you back when I know something."

After finishing on the phone, Brian sat in a daze, frozen in his workout gear, while the others showered and dressed for lunch. He would soon catch up with them. For now, though, he had way too much on his mind to care about food.

Brian was still stewing about his bad snap when he joined his fellow job candidates in the team cafeteria. Wanting to be alone with his thoughts, Brian sat apart from the others. He intentionally faced the entrance to the dining area because he wanted to keep an eye out for the head honchos: Belichick and personnel boss Scott Pioli. They soon walked in together and headed straight to Brian. Standing to greet them, Brian did not know if this was simply going to be the "hello" Pioli had promised or if he was about to learn his fate. Belichick and Pioli offered smiles and handshakes, and the initial conversation was entirely casual. While the other three long snappers continued eating, or at least fidgeted with their food while anxiously eavesdropping, Belichick and Brian exchanged updates about their wives and children. In Cleveland, Belichick had been friendly with Lori Kinchen, who was routinely around the team facility in her role as president of the Browns wives' association. In fact, she had often dropped into Belichick's office just to chat, which almost nobody ever did; given a choice, most insiders generally preferred to avoid the blunt and standoffish coach because he intimidated them. Although still not much of a contender to be voted Mr. Congeniality, Belichick now seemed genuinely pleased to hear that Lori and the Kinchen boys were all doing well back in Louisiana.

It soon became clear, though, that Belichick had more than small talk on his agenda. When the conversation shifted to the tryout, he told Brian, "Looked like you did pretty well."

Instead of saying anything about the bad snap—even trying to explain it away would only draw attention to a negative—Brian wanted to stay as upbeat and light as possible: "Not bad for an old man, huh?"

"Yeah, well, looks like you're in pretty good shape," Belichick said.

Brian still had no idea where the conversation was headed. He and Belichick spoke about how well the Patriots had been doing and about the challenges that remained—including the assimilation of a new long snapper only a couple of weeks before facing the do-or-die pressure of the NFL playoffs.

"It's not exactly the best of timing," Brian said. "I mean, whoever you choose will probably have the team's entire season in his hands at some point."

"You know what?" Belichick said with absolute nonchalance. "You're going to be that guy."

"Really?" Brian said.

"Let's get this done," Belichick said. "You have an agent you want us to call?"

That was the full extent of Brian's official invitation back onto the grand stage of the NFL—no bells and whistles, no lavish pronouncement, only matter-of-fact logistics. That was also how the other three long snappers learned—by overhearing the conversation—that they were about to be sent home.

Brian told Belichick and Pioli there was no need for an agent. He had been out of football for three years, had long since abandoned the idea of ever being back in the game, and now he was being asked to join a championship-caliber team that was beating everyone in sight. He certainly was not about to quibble over contract terms. He just wanted to call Lori.

"She's waiting to hear from me," Brian said.

"Well, why don't you go ahead and call her and let me say hello," Belichick said.

Lori was in a classroom at Parkview Baptist—it was the last day of review with Brian's students before the big end-of-semester exam—when her cell phone rang. A good number of the kids jumped out of their seats and rushed up to surround her desk for the moment of truth.

"Hey," Lori said into the phone. "Have you heard anything?"

"Hold on," Brian said. "Somebody wants to talk to you."

Lori immediately recognized Belichick's voice. "Long time, no see," he said.

"I know, it's been a long time," Lori said.

"Well, looks like I'll be seeing you soon."

"Where?"

"When you come up here to see your husband," Belichick said.

"What?" Lori screamed into the phone. "He made it?"

"We're signing him."

Lori made no attempt to contain herself.

"He made it!" she shouted to the students. "Oh, my gosh, he made it!"

The students exploded with clapping and screaming. For the second day in a row, pandemonium temporarily ruled the classroom. Everyone was so happy for Brian. The students were also thrilled that they now knew a professional football player. A few of the boys immediately declared the Patriots their new favorite team. One of the girls wanted to know if Brian had met Tom Brady, the star quarterback with the *GQ* looks. (He had not—not yet.)

When the class ended, Lori rushed off to the school office and shared the exciting news with everyone. Other than offering the standard morning announcements and a prayer to start each day, principal Cooper Pope generally exercised restraint when it came to school-wide broadcasting over the intercom. This time he did not hesitate. With so many people at Parkview, both students and staff, waiting to hear about Brian's tryout, Pope was eager to share the outcome. "I know that all of you are wondering how Coach Kinchen is doing in New England," he said into the microphone. "We just got a call from him. For your information, Coach Kinchen is now a New England Patriot. We need to be sure to watch him on TV this weekend. We need to keep pulling for him and to keep praying for him."

While the Louisiana school buzzed with excitement, Brian sat in an office at the Patriots headquarters and looked over his contract. He at least skimmed the twenty-five paragraphs of legal gobbledygook in the standard NFL contract and the three additional clauses in a one-page attachment prepared by the Patriots. But he was not really concerned about any of it. He would be paid based on what was then the minimum annual salary—$755,000— for a player with thirteen years of NFL experience. Prorated over the course of the seventeen-week season, sixteen games plus a bye week, that came to $44,411.76 for each of the two games left in the regular season. (In two weeks, Brian would be paid more than triple his annual salary as a first-year teacher.) Playoff money would be on top of that. But the bottom line for Brian had nothing to do with financial compensation. Only one thing really mattered: he was back in the National Football League . . . starting fresh with a team that had everything going for it. By putting blue ink to paper, signing both the contract and the attachment, Brian instantly became the oldest member of the New England Patriots. He also became the only NFL player who just the day before had been working in a classroom—studying the Bible—with a bunch of seventh graders.

Pioli's secretary gave Brian the team's mailing address so that Lori could ship clothes to him overnight. All he needed now was calories. Brian was already thinking about the size and strength of the behemoths he would soon be battling on the football field—and about the disadvantage he'd be facing because of the twenty-plus pounds he had lost since leaving the NFL. With that in mind, he had one more stop to make before heading to a hotel for the rest of the day. Brian returned to the team cafeteria and loaded his bag with an arsenal of junk food: Candy bars. Cookies. Bottles of chocolate and strawberry Nestle Quik milk drinks—as many calories as he could fit in his bag. His motivation made perfect sense: *I've got to start getting heavier or I'm going to get abused.*

Four

He never aspired to be a long snapper, never even once thought about the possibility while growing up. And why would he have? Brian was way too athletic, way too driven, to ever contemplate being relegated to such a limited role. In his earliest days of organized football—Saturday mornings playing for the South Baton Rouge Tigers in a local youth league—eight-year-old Brian was a one-boy wrecking crew. It was only because his father was coaching that Brian was even allowed to play at such a young age. Most of the other boys on the team, including Brian's big brother, Cal, were ten. But age meant nothing once the action began.

Gus Kinchen put Brian on the defensive line at middle guard—a position now called nose tackle—and the youngest boy on the team immediately stood out because he reacted so quickly to the snap of the ball. Brian was never going to be the fastest kid in a footrace. But what he lacked in pure speed he more than made up for with great anticipation and remarkable reflexes. Sometimes he responded so well to the first movement of the center that he could stop a play before it had any chance of developing—getting the center and the quarterback all jammed up while they were exchanging the ball.

It made no difference whether Brian was only practicing during the week or going full throttle in a game on Saturday. He simply loved putting on his football gear and making something happen. Nobody ever had to teach him that; he was instinctively drawn to the entire football experience. Maybe it was somehow ingrained in him because of his family background. Perhaps it was purely the love of competition—a boy just being a boy, wanting to go head-to-head with the other boys and wanting to be better than everyone else. Whatever it was, Brian was always the aggressor on a football field. He was never scared of contact. He loved hitting people, loved trying to barrel through anyone in his way.

Both on and off the field, Brian was quite stubborn. One of the best ways to get him to do something was to tell him that he could not. Yet he was also extremely shy and quiet. He often lacked confidence. One day in grade school, a teacher gave Brian and his classmates an assignment to write about why they were important. "I am important because God made me important," Brian wrote. "I am important because I want to be important. I am important because I try to be important. I am important because my parents teach me to be important." Despite such bold statements, though, Brian was never really that sure of his place in the world. Much later, as an adult with children of his own, he would reflect on his youth and conclude that he had been a classic middle child: never getting as much parental attention as he wanted, always yearning for more, constantly seeking recognition by way of achievement. As much as he enjoyed sports for the pure bliss of physical activity and the sheer fun of playing games with his friends, Brian also craved— and then relished—the affirmation that came with outstanding performance. "Great job," someone would tell him after a football game or a tennis match or whatever he was into at the time, and then those simple words of praise could easily spend hours, if not days, dancing in his head. No doubt about it: those words were fuel for his engine.

By the time he entered high school, Brian had already excelled at any sport he took up: Football. Basketball. Swimming. Golf. Tennis. Track and field. Friends and teammates knew that Brian was an unusually gifted athlete. But they also marveled at his drive to keep working and keep improving. On top of everything else, Brian was extremely analytical—always trying to figure out the ideal form or the perfect motion or whatever he needed to adjust so that he could do something better than he was already doing it.

Decades later, followers of the local sports scene would still shake their heads at what Brian did as a high school senior in the 1983 Class A state championships of track and field. He set a state record in the shot put and also won the discus. He placed second in the high jump and sixth in the javelin. And he did all of that in a single day. Brian was the only athlete from University High School who even qualified for the meet, but his solo efforts in the field events were enough to propel his "team" to first place in the overall standings prior to the running events (in which he did not compete). The twenty-nine points he personally accumulated ultimately placed U-High seventh in the meet. With the passing of years, the story would only get better. Legend would eventually have it that Brian won the entire state meet all by himself. It was not true, but so what? It was only a track-and-field story. Anyone in Louisiana knows that football is the only sport that really matters.

Football was certainly top priority for Brian. His goals were always clear: Play well enough in high school to follow in his father's footsteps by earning a football scholarship to LSU. Then shine in college and be drafted into the NFL—preferably by his favorite team, the Miami Dolphins, whose Hall of Fame fullback, Larry Csonka, was the one player he had always admired the most. "Hard, tough, no-nonsense guy," Brian would tell friends. "That's who I want to be like."

It did not take long for Brian to gain recognition for his own no-nonsense approach to the game. Three straight years, starting as a high school sophomore, he was named an All-State linebacker. Teammates had a more personal but equally telling label for him: Super Kinch. As a senior, playing both linebacker on defense and fullback on offense, Brian led U-High to the Class A state championship game. Schools all over the country—Notre Dame, UCLA, Texas A&M, and Duke, among them—expressed interest in his services. But none of them had a chance. On February 1, 1983, with college football's national signing day coming the next week, the LSU coaching staff sent Brian a Western Union Mailgram with an abbreviated version of what they had already been telling him for quite some time: "LSU fans everywhere are talking about you. We want to see you playing in Tiger Stadium." Eight days later, Brian was one of twenty-one players who signed national letters of intent to join the LSU Tigers.

It was one of the greatest days of his young life—and how could it not have been? He had grown up hearing so many stories about the 1958 national championship team. He had spent so many Saturdays tailgating outside the stadium with family and friends. He had always worn the purple and gold of LSU. And Brian knew the way everyone around Baton Rouge followed LSU football, the way everyone loved LSU football. So where else could he possibly want to be?

For the people of a state that has historically absorbed national-image beatings for an ugly plethora of ills such as racism, dirty politics, and bad schools, LSU football has long served as something of an elixir, a common bond that goes way beyond any weekly measurement of points on a scoreboard. LSU football brings people together and lifts the collective spirit. It offers a chance to be among the best at something. And even when the Tigers might be having an off year, well, clearly nobody likes that, but the games are still top priority on calendars all over Louisiana. Of course, LSU fans do not rally around their players and coaches only during the season; they scrutinize and worship The Program (always capitalized) all year long. Even Huey Long, the celebrated governor and U.S. senator known as the Kingfish, could not help but inject himself into the minutiae of LSU football back in the 1920s and 1930s. He assisted with recruiting and routinely offered advice on everything from personnel moves to the marching band. According to a biography by renowned historian T. Harry Williams, Long once told one of the coaches, "LSU can't have a losing team because that'll mean I'm associated with a loser."

Through the years, countless ordinary LSU fans have been equally passionate about their Tigers. That is why they incessantly put vocal chords at risk by pelting rival teams and their followers with screams of "Tiger bait, Tiger bait." It is why legendary Alabama coach Bear

Bryant once described Baton Rouge as the worst place in the world for a visiting team—"like being inside a drum," he said—and why Tiger Stadium became commonly known as Death Valley. It also explains how the standard LSU football game was long ago transformed from mere sporting event into full-scale cultural spectacle. With home games traditionally played under the lights on Saturday nights, tailgating goes all day long and covers not only stadium parking lots but also significant chunks of campus. This is a major social event—"the best pre-game party in the country," ESPN has declared it. Trailing only Mardi Gras and perhaps Jazz Fest, it is one of the biggest bashes in the state, with close to a hundred thousand people gathering in temporary community and never without ample supply of adult beverages. And to think: all of this revelry revolves around a bunch of college athletes—kids playing games! LSU football players are treated like absolute royalty.

In his memoir *It Never Rains in Tiger Stadium,* a former LSU captain named John Ed Bradley offers a telling exchange he once shared with a teammate, Marty Dufrene, an offensive lineman from Lafourche Parish (in Cajun Country), long after their playing days had ended.

"Nothing I've ever experienced compares to that first time I ran out with the team as a freshman—out into Tiger Stadium," Dufrene told Bradley. "God, I was fifteen feet off the ground and covered with *frissons.* You know what *frissons* are, John Ed? They're goose bumps. It's the French word for goose bumps. It was the highest high you could have, and no drugs could match it—the way it felt to run out there with the crowd standing and yelling for you. I wish every kid could experience that."

"If every kid could," Bradley responded to Dufrene, "then it wouldn't be what it is. It's because so few get there that it has such power."

As one of the few, Brian Kinchen arrived at LSU wanting to quickly establish himself as a linebacker who would contribute in big ways. But a coaching decision abruptly ended any chance of that: Brian was "redshirted" as a freshman, meaning he would practice with the team but would not play in games. This was a fairly common practice that allowed a not-ready-for-prime-time newcomer to get acclimated while still maintaining his four years of collegiate playing eligibility. The expectation was that Brian would now spend five years instead of four at LSU. It was not what Brian wanted: he wanted to play right away. But there was nothing he could do about it.

As significant as the redshirt decision seemed at the time, though, head coach Jerry Stovall made another move that would ultimately have a far more dramatic impact on Brian's college experience and even on the entire course of his adult life. Stovall moved Brian from defense to offense—from linebacker to tight end—because a couple of guys were hurt and someone needed to fill in during practices. Brian was a good choice, Stovall felt, because he had both the athletic ability to excel at his new position and the character to put the team first and do whatever was asked of him. There was an old saying that had long made the rounds in football circles—and that Brian now started hearing for the first time at LSU: "The more things you can do, the better chance you have of sticking around." Brian did not only stick around at tight end. He excelled to the point that the offensive coaches never gave him back to the defense. Stovall was not surprised. To him, Brian was "a real warrior" who always responded well to a challenge.

That also became the consensus of others who coached and played at LSU. An in-house scouting report on Brian would have read something like this: "Fierce competitor. Nobody outworks him. Relentless when blocking. Great hands when catching passes. Makes up for lack of speed with excellent routes and technique. Plays hurt. Quiet but confident. Strong. Tough. Intense."

"Brian was a much better athlete than most guys that played tight end—that's what stood out," recalls Ed Zaunbrecher, then LSU's offensive coordinator. "You couldn't measure his value just based on his numbers. He helped us with a lot of things that would never show up in the numbers."

His junior season—1986—offered perfect illustration of that. Brian caught twenty-seven passes for 262 yards and four touchdowns, certainly not eye-popping statistics in an offense that broke the school record for total yards in a season and led the Tigers to the Southeastern Conference championship. Yet Brian impressed a lot of people: he was named first-team All-Conference and honorable mention All-American. So much for numbers. His childhood dream of playing in the NFL seemed within reach.

One day at practice, LSU assistant coach Terry Lewis, who worked with the tight ends, pulled Brian aside and asked him if he had ever tried long snapping. Lewis enjoyed teaching the specialty skill, especially when he could handpick someone who might be able to snap on punts and would also be athletic enough to then get down the field to help with coverage. Lewis knew how Brian used to hit as a linebacker and had always been impressed by the way he attacked defenders as a tight end. Why not see if he could contribute on special teams as well?

"Never snapped in my life," Brian told Lewis. But he was willing to try.

"It's simply passing the ball between your legs," Lewis assured his new pupil. "Same way a quarterback throws it."

Well, not exactly. Lewis started with instructions for gripping the ball: Grab it comfortably with your right hand, your dominant hand, cupping the ball, with your ring finger on the third lace. This is your throwing hand, and you want it underneath the ball, with the seam opposite the laces staring you right in the face. Your left hand, the guide hand, goes just to the left of that seam, with your thumb parallel to it.

"It feels pretty awkward," Brian said.

"Always does when you're just starting out," Lewis said. "You'll get used to it."

Next came basic coaching points for proper stance when leaning over the ball: You want your feet spread a little wider than shoulder width. You can have a slight stagger—with the dominant foot back just a bit—if that feels better and helps with balance. You want to push your big toes down into the ground, maybe even causing slight daylight under your heels. Got to have a little flex in the knees. That will help you keep your butt down. Must keep that butt low or the ball will go flying too high. Extend your arms as far out as possible to create space between your body and the defensive lineman on your nose, but without reaching beyond the point of comfort.

And as far as the snap itself: You don't want to pick up the ball and throw it. Just pull it straight back between your legs—firing back with elbows inside your knees—and then release. Aim by extending your hands toward the target, thumbs turning out from the body as you extend and release.

"You're going to be a little erratic at first," Lewis told Brian. "It's just one of those things that you have to practice, practice, practice."

Brian was already plenty busy working with the offense during LSU practices. And teammate Chris Carrier, a defensive back, was firmly entrenched as the LSU long snapper. From time to time, though, Brian worked on snapping off to the side while the first-team punt unit went through its practice repetitions. With Lewis encouraging him, Brian became fairly proficient, and he was eventually asked to snap during a team scrimmage.

When the time finally came for him to deliver a football to a real punter at full speed and with bodies crashing all around him, Brian went through all the same mechanics that had come to feel pretty routine and comfortable. Or at least he thought he did. Alas, once released from his hands, the football took two ugly hops and skidded along the ground before the punter could even take a stab at it. The experiment was over. Brian continued to dabble with snapping when he had nothing better to do. But he never got another chance to snap with the LSU punt team. Not even in practice.

Brian still had a slew of significant moments ahead of him, however. The most memorable personal highlight of his college career came during his final season, in a nationally televised showdown against conference rival Georgia. LSU went into the game undefeated (four wins and a tie) and ranked seventh in the country. Georgia was ranked sixteenth and playing in front of a frenzied home crowd of 82,122. Trailing 23–19 late in the fourth quarter, LSU marched the ball down the field. On second-and-goal at the Georgia five-yard line, the Tigers went to a play called "Cougar," which involved a fake handoff and two tight ends trying to further confuse the defense by crossing. As the play was designed, quarterback Tommy Hodson's first two choices were passing to either tailback Sammy Martin in the right flat or tight end Willie Williams in the right side of the end zone. But neither option opened up. Hodson looked for the third choice in his progression . . . and there he was. After crossing from right to left, Brian was open about midway into the end zone. Hodson threw him the ball and Brian made a leaping catch. Touchdown! With 3:36 left on the clock, LSU had the winning points and Brian had the signature play of his college years.

A week later, his good fortune turned to bad. Playing against Kentucky in Tiger Stadium, Brian was engaged in a block when one of his teammates unintentionally rammed into him. Brian went down with a broken left leg, and LSU announced that it would cost him the remainder of the season. It did not. Determined not to let a fractured fibula define the end of his LSU football journey, Brian was back in action five weeks later against Tulane. He also played in LSU's 30–13 Gator Bowl victory over South Carolina—capping off both his college career and a tremendous four-year run for the Tigers. From 1984 through 1987, their cumulative record was 36–9–3. After the fourth game of the 1984 season, they never again entered a game without being ranked among the top twenty teams in the nation. And during each of those years they spent at least a couple of weeks in the top ten—climbing as high as number four in 1987.

Although Brian was never able to match his dad's LSU football legacy by winning a national championship, the father-son symmetry took on two other forms. The first came when Brian's younger brother, Todd, signed with LSU to play football, just as Gus Kinchen's younger brother, Gary, had done more than a quarter of a century earlier. When Brian was a fifth-year senior and Todd was a redshirt freshman, they made local sports history. Never before had pairs of brothers from two generations of a Baton Rouge family played for the Tigers. Todd went on to a stellar college career as a wide receiver and kick returner, twice being named All-Southeastern Conference, and then played in the NFL for seven years. Writing about the four football-playing Kinchens in his book *Game of My Life: LSU*—and noting that Brian and Todd's mom was a cheerleader and twice the Darling of LSU—author Marty Mulé refers to the Kinchens as the First Family of LSU football. And that is without any mention of the second major parallel between the LSU experiences of father Gus and son Brian. Mulé says nothing of the fact that Brian also ended up with a head-turning cheerleader—and that the girl he would later marry was even part of the first LSU cheerleading squad to win a national championship of its own.

They met soon after Brian broke his leg. He was on crutches, slowly working his way from Broussard Hall, the football dorm, over to the stadium, when he crossed paths with a shapely brunette who happened to be waiting for a friend outside a classroom building.

"Hey, how's your leg?" she blurted out.

"Oh, it's okay," Brian said. "I'm going for treatment."

"Hope you feel better."

"Thanks."

And that was it. Brian was stunned that such a beautiful girl had initiated conversation with him. He was much more accustomed to the best-looking girls playing what he called "the hard-to-get card" and staying to themselves unless first showered with attention. Maybe part of it was the fact that he was not the most confident of guys around the girls. Working his way down the hill toward Tiger Stadium, Brian knew exactly what he had to do. He had to find Tommy Hodson. The star quarterback was much more involved in the LSU social scene than he was. Maybe Tommy could help him figure out who that girl was . . . and if he might even be able to get a date with her.

Meanwhile, Lori Commagere could not believe she had finally spoken to Brian, even though it was only a brief exchange and he still had no clue who she was. She thought back to a time four years earlier—when she was just a high school freshman and Brian was a freshman at LSU—when she first noticed him. Actually, it was only a small head shot in the LSU football program that caught her attention. Lori was at an LSU game with friends from her hometown of Lafayette, Louisiana, and she immediately declared Brian both the cutest guy on the team and her future boyfriend. "I'll just meet him when I get to LSU," she said. One of the other girls countered with a harsh reality check: "If you ever go to LSU, he won't even be there anymore." But then someone explained to Lori that Brian was not actually playing that season because he was being redshirted. Therefore, they could conceivably be on the same campus for a year. "See," Lori said to her friends. It never even dawned on her that Brian might already have a girlfriend. Or that he might by the time she arrived on the scene. Or that he might not be the least bit interested in some random girl who was then just a ninth grader.

Crutching his way into the locker room four years after Lori had gone to that game, Brian went straight to Tommy Hodson and explained what had just happened. Tommy had never seen his friend so excited about a girl.

"Don't worry," Tommy said. "We'll find out who she is. What did she look like?"

"Pretty short," Brian said. "Black hair. Great body. Really fit and athletic looking. Big smile. The whole package."

Tommy laughed. "I love the description," he said. "Doesn't exactly help us narrow it down, though."

The conundrum continued until the next weekend, when LSU played Ole Miss in Jackson, Mississippi. Despite being out of action with his bad leg, Brian made the trip with the team. Ranked fifth in the country, LSU easily won the game, 42–13, but it was not until time had expired that Brian unexpectedly scored his most meaningful victory of the day. It came right after the post-game prayer—players and cheerleaders from both teams huddled in the middle of the field—when Brian looked up and locked eyes with his mystery girl. She was a cheerleader!

"Hey," Lori said.

"Hey," Brian said.

He was still too timid to start an actual conversation. He once again walked off without even getting her name. But this time Brian at least knew how to find out who she was and track her down if ever he could gather the courage to ask her out. He soon went to one of his Sigma Chi fraternity brothers, Greg Sample, who was also a cheerleader, and learned Lori's name. It was a good start, but Brian also wanted a reconnaissance report. He had dated the same girl for six years, three in high school and three in college, and even after that relationship ended, he had typically gone out only with girls he already knew pretty well. As a result, he had almost no experience with the uncertainty of asking out someone new, and the fear of being rejected was simply too much for him. Fortunately for Brian, Greg was willing to play the junior-high-like role of go-between and soon delivered the news Brian wanted to hear. Yes, all he needed to do was ask, and Lori would be happy to go on a date.

Brian finally called. They went to dinner and a movie—*Nuts* with Barbra Streisand—and he could not believe how easily the conversation flowed. Lori was fun and funny. She was confident yet down-to-earth. Brian felt like he was out with an old friend. Lori was truly amazed that her frivolous ninth-grade fantasy might actually be coming to fruition.

Their lives would never again be the same.

By the spring of his fifth year at LSU—with a new relationship blooming and classes finally winding down—only one major item remained on Brian's college to-do list: get picked in the NFL draft. The idea of playing football at the highest level—the challenge of competing against the biggest, strongest, fastest players in the world—was by itself enough of a draw for him. But Brian also saw the money and the status that went with playing in the NFL, and he was equally drawn to the possibility that being a professional football player would somehow make him feel whole as a man. Brian was not yet using the word *validation* when thinking and talking about what it would mean to become a big-time player in the NFL, but the general concept was nonetheless intertwined with his NFL dreams and aspirations.

The afternoon of Sunday, April 24, 1988, Brian hunkered down in front of a television at his grandparents' Baton Rouge home and watched early coverage of the draft from the Marriott Marquis in New York. Not that he was expecting to see his name called during the live broadcast of the earliest selections. ESPN's coverage would be long done by the time he was hoping to be picked, in the fourth or fifth round. But this was a good way to get in the mood and build up to the moment he'd been working toward for years. Then he would sit by a telephone and wait for someone to call from one of the twenty-eight teams then in the NFL. There was only one problem: nobody called. Five rounds of picks were made that day. Seven tight ends were selected. But the knocks on Brian—that he might be too small and too slow to thrive at tight end in the NFL—were clearly hurting him more than he had anticipated. He would have to wait for the second day of the draft.

After a restless night, Brian began the next morning with a workout at LSU. When he returned to his grandparents' house, he was surprised to find a scout from the Dallas Cowboys waiting for him. The scout wanted him to know that if he was not selected in the remaining seven rounds of the draft, the Cowboys would be interested in signing him as a free agent. Perhaps Brian should have been pleased that someone wanted him. But his reaction—kept to himself as best he could—was the complete opposite. *Does this guy actually think I'm not going to be drafted? I'm good enough that the Cowboys want me as a free agent but not good enough for them to use a draft pick on me?* Brian was even more upset than he had been the night before.

The scout left, and hours passed without any activity. When the phone finally rang, it was Kurt Schottenheimer, a former LSU assistant coach then with the Cleveland Browns. Brian was happy to hear from someone he knew. The good news was that the Browns were thinking about picking him. The bad news was that the draft was already in the ninth round. Brian could hardly believe it. "Sit tight," Schottenheimer told him. "Don't go anywhere." But the Browns never called again. Brian went from frustrated to fuming. After a while, he stormed out of the house and went to play golf— anything to get his mind off the minute-by-minute deterioration of his hopes and dreams.

Brian had just hit an approach shot to the fifth green when he saw his brother Cal running across an adjacent fairway, calling out to him: "You were drafted. Miami Dolphins!" Brian's favorite team of all time—how could it be any better than that?

"Awesome," Brian said. "What round?"

"Twelfth."

So much for the joy of the moment.

"Oh, come on," Brian said. "You're kidding me."

Cal was not kidding.

"Mr. Irrelevant" is the title playfully awarded each year to the last player taken in the NFL draft. As the 320th selection, Brian was only thirteen picks from being tagged with that moniker. With his ego bruised, Brian would begin training camp with the Dolphins as a long shot to make it in the NFL. Clearly, this was not the ideal point of entry for someone who sought his affirmation in the unforgiving, win-or-lose world of professional sports.

Five

His initial road trip as a professional athlete would have been quite memorable even without playing any football, because the Dolphins went to London for their first pre-season game of 1988. Brian had never been to Europe. Now he and his jet-lagged teammates were visiting Windsor Castle and checking out Big Ben. But the Dolphins did not cross the Atlantic Ocean only to see the attractions; with the NFL trying to expand its international appeal, they also *were* an attraction. They played the San Francisco 49ers the evening of Sunday, July 31, at Wembley Stadium. Both teams offered extraordinary headliners. Don Shula of the Dolphins and Bill Walsh of the 49ers were among the most-acclaimed coaches in football history. And they were accompanied by five players who would later join them in the Pro Football Hall of Fame: Dan Marino of the Dolphins; Joe Montana, Steve Young, Jerry Rice, and Ronnie Lott of the 49ers. Of course, an early pre-season game was never actually about the star players. They would make only cameo appearances. This was really a chance for untested rookies and borderline veterans to show why they deserved to be kept for the regular season.

Brian was assigned to play on the kick-coverage unit. And he was slated for limited time at tight end in the fourth quarter once veteran starter Bruce Hardy and fellow rookie Ferrell Edmunds were done for the night. Brian ended up with a solid showing in both roles, making a few good hits while covering kicks, and hauling in a fifteen-yard reception on a critical third-down play that set up the winning touchdown late in the fourth quarter. *Not a bad start,* he told himself. *Got to keep doing stuff like that if I'm gonna make this team.*

But the most significant development for Brian in the Dolphins' come-from-behind victory (27–21) had nothing to do with his own performance. It happened on the opening kickoff. Charging downfield on the Miami coverage team, reserve linebacker Scott Nicolas was hammered on a hit he never saw coming. The six-year NFL veteran went down with considerable damage to his right knee and would never again play. That left a critical void: Nicolas had also been the snapper on the Miami punt team. (Starting center Jeff Dellenbach snapped for field goals and extra points, but Shula preferred to use a more athletic player for punt snaps, someone who could not only snap and block but also sprint downfield and make a tackle.) Bruce Hardy took on the job for the game in London. But that was only a short-term fix: Hardy was an eleventh-year veteran whose career was winding down. Once the Dolphins were back on American soil, Shula would want to find a younger guy who could snap for punts. As it turned out, he already had one in the Miami training camp.

In the silence of his mind, Brian had never stopped hearing that old football adage to which he had been introduced at LSU: *The more things you can do, the better chance you have of sticking around.* With those words as motivation, he had decided to do some snapping in practices with the Dolphins. At the time, each NFL team could keep only forty-five men on its roster, so few teams could afford the luxury of dedicating a slot to someone who was strictly a snapper. The evolution of the snapper to a full-time specialty job would not come until years later with the expansion of rosters—eventually, in 1994, to the current limit of fifty-three men. For now, though, Brian was just thinking that any little extra might help his chances of survival. So what if he had never even snapped in a game? He knew that Shula liked taking a good athlete and finding something new for him to do. *Versatility* had long been a catchword in the Miami locker room.

The week after playing in London, the Dolphins had their second pre-season game, in Chicago against the Bears. At the team hotel the morning of the game, special-teams coach Mike Westhoff told Brian that he would be the punt snapper that night. Brian quickly concluded: *If I can do this well, I'm going to make the team.* The thought both excited him and made him nervous. But he snapped the ball well—four straight strikes to punter Reggie Roby—in the Dolphins' 20–17 loss to the Bears.

Brian kept snapping throughout training camp and in all the pre-season games. He did not possess all the tools that Shula generally looked for in a tight end, most notably the ideal size and speed, but the veteran coach was still impressed. He saw Brian as a very intelligent guy who worked hard, always tried to do the right things, and seldom made mistakes. Of course, fighting against the odds of being a last-round pick, Brian still needed to show that he could contribute something special. "Snapping was probably the biggest factor," Shula would later remember. "Brian was very dependable. We had a lot of confidence in him."

When the time came for final roster cuts, nobody on the coaching staff said a word to Brian, which he took to mean that he should keep showing up for work. He was right. The depth chart showed him as first-team punt snapper and third-string tight end. Brian was officially a member of the Miami Dolphins—a full-fledged player in the National Football League. "Not a lot of people can say that their boyhood dreams have come true in life," he told an Associated Press writer. "Right now, mine has."

Brian snapped well for the punt team. Late in his second season, he also started snapping for field goals and extra points. But he got almost no action on offense. In three seasons with the Dolphins, he caught a grand total of two passes for fifteen yards. In the beginning, just making the team and being stamped "professional football player" had given him such a sense of accomplishment. But now he wanted all his hard work to pay off with something more. Brian wanted to be a go-to guy in the passing game, routinely hauling in passes and lighting up the scoreboard with touchdowns. That was not going to happen in Miami. After the 1990 season, when Shula had to select which players to protect and which to leave exposed on the free-agent market, Brian was deemed expendable. As challenging as his initial years in the NFL had been—always feeling like he worked his tail off but never really knowing where he stood with his coaches and the front office—this was the first time Brian directly experienced the harshest realities of being a professional athlete who existed on the fringe: In his third year of marriage, Brian had no clue where he and Lori would next live. He had no idea if another team would offer any greater opportunity to make a meaningful mark . . . or whether his next stop would provide any job security at all.

The Green Bay Packers invited Brian for a workout and tickled his eardrums with everything he wanted to hear. They wanted him—and he would not even need to be the long snapper. Yes, they would be happy to have him in case something happened to veteran snapper Blair Bush. But what they really wanted Brian to do was play tight end. The Packers had played with only two tight ends for most of the 1990 season. Now they wanted a third. Brian signed a contract and happily joined the Packers. Everything seemed to be going well in training camp. But on Monday, August 26, 1991, six days before the season opener, Brian had an unexpected visitor to his dorm room. Every player in the NFL knows exactly what is meant by the words "Coach wants to see you. Bring your playbook." It means you are leaving. Brian now heard those dreaded words. Coach Lindy Infante had changed his mind and decided to keep only two tight ends. Brian was released.

Driving home to Baton Rouge, he was angry about the way he had been treated. After telling him that they were going to keep three tight ends—and after using that information as an enticement for Brian to sign with them—the Packers had abruptly abandoned that plan and put him out on the street. Still, Brian was not overly dejected. *No big deal,* he kept telling himself. *I'll still be picked up by another team.*

But when a couple of weeks passed without anyone calling for his services, Brian worried. He certainly did not want to think his NFL career was crashing to a halt after only three years simply because one team had decided to go with two tight ends instead of three. And he and Lori had just bought their first house. With little Austin not yet two years old and Lori pregnant again, Brian was not only stressed about his football career. He was also concerned about finances.

Then a Cleveland Browns linebacker named Randy Kirk, who doubled as a long snapper, pulled a hamstring. Eighteen days after being cut by the Packers, Brian was in Cleveland, trying out for a team led by first-year head coach Bill Belichick. Two days later, Brian went to work for the Browns in their third game of the 1991 season, a home game against the Cincinnati Bengals. Late in the second quarter, with the Browns leading, 5–3, Brian set up with holder Brian Hansen and kicker Matt Stover for a fairly easy field-goal attempt from thirty-four yards out. But Brian threw a low snap and Stover never got off a kick. *We lose this game, and I'm history,* Brian figured. And, no matter what might happen with the score, he was now faced with an unforgiving reality for the remainder of the afternoon: *I mess up again, and there's no way they keep me here.* Amazingly enough, the game ultimately came down to a last-minute field-goal attempt. With nine seconds left and the Browns trailing, 13–11, they lined up to try a forty-five-yard field goal for the win. Brian was not the only one feeling the pressure. It was Stover's first year kicking in the NFL, and this was his first shot at a game-winner. "I'm out there just about pooping in my pants," Stover would later admit. "But Brian snaps a bull's-eye. Perfect hold.

And I nail it." The Browns and their fans wildly celebrated a 14–13 victory—and Brian kept his job.

In fact, he soon gained a firm hold on his position with the Browns. Special-teams coach Scott O'Brien came to count on him not only for his accuracy as a snapper, but also for what he contributed in other ways. O'Brien generally relied on a player he called "the personal protector" to make calls and direct the blocking scheme once everyone was lined up for a punt. As the only player between the offensive line and the punter, the personal protector (or "PP") was the punter's final hope for security against anyone who might otherwise threaten him with the possibility of a punt block. But the PP was also responsible for shouting out protection calls and making adjustments, because he was in the best position to see how the other team was setting up to attack. O'Brien noticed that Brian was often somehow a step ahead of the PP, and he began to think of his snapper almost like a coach on the field. There was one other attribute Brian brought to the punt team. He was among the best at his position when it came to getting down the field and making a tackle. O'Brien wished he had more guys with Brian's toughness and intensity.

Once Brian was secure with his job as a snapper, he wanted more work at tight end. He practiced hard and lobbied to play on offense. But the Browns always found someone bigger or faster—or both—to put ahead of him. In 1992, Belichick even brought in former New York Giants All-Pro Mark Bavaro, a two-time Super Bowl champion who was by then battling a degenerative knee condition. Bavaro had not been able to play the previous season, and his doctor had advised him to retire. But Belichick wanted him. Though the arrival of Bavaro meant yet another year without Brian catching a single pass—his third consecutive season with no receptions—the two became good friends. Both were deeply spiritual, pretty quiet and reserved away from the field, but once they put on their pads and helmets, they were two of the most aggressive guys on the team. Brian enjoyed Bavaro's company and learned a lot from him. He also liked to give Bavaro a hard time—always in fun, but sometimes with a bit of envy and attitude as well—because Bavaro missed so many practices to rest his bad knee.

"You're not practicing *again*?" Brian would ask in the locker room. "Must be nice."

Then Bavaro would hobble off to the training room while Brian joined the other backup tight end, Scott Galbraith, on the practice field, always stuck with the grunt work throughout the week even though Bavaro would inevitably be the starter and get the vast majority of playing time on game days. It was almost like Bavaro had two jobs that season. One was to get his body ready for the games—that knee was extremely painful. And the other was to put up with all of Brian's barbs and snipes. Bavaro knew that the situation could cause tension. But he and Brian actually enjoyed the give-and-take that came with the unusual dynamics of their relationship. Although the teasing was a constant, Bavaro very much appreciated the encouragement he also got from Brian. In return, Bavaro kept assuring Brian that his time at tight end was going to come. He was young. He was a good player. And Bavaro knew that his own stay with the Browns was not going to last long.

Bavaro was indeed gone after one season in Cleveland. Even so, Brian expected that the Browns would again dash his hopes by bringing in someone new to play ahead of him. But he got off to a good start in training camp during the summer of 1993, and Belichick was ready to give him the chance he had always wanted. With his sixth NFL season approaching, Brian was finally informed that he would be a first-team player on offense—the starting tight end!

Brian was not the only person deeply moved by the news. His dad had always shared from afar the emotional challenges that came with being a peripheral player. Gus Kinchen could certainly relate to the frustration of consistently longing for something more. He, too, had experienced a significant amount of job-related stress, having spent most of his adult years in what he defined as "an up-and-down business life" working for IBM and others. But business had lost its appeal as other priorities took hold of him. Gus eventually went to a seminary in Mississippi and then became a youth minister back in Baton Rouge. Now he was working as area director for the Fellowship of Christian Athletes. When Brian called to tell his dad that the starting job was at long last his, Gus was naturally overjoyed, and he could not help but reflect. He thought about Brian's terrible disappointment during draft weekend in 1988. He thought about everything his son had endured en route to achieving his long-coveted goal of being a starter: The mental anguish. The physical grind. All the waiting and the hoping.

Gus was not one to get overly emotional with his children. But he wanted to express how very proud he was of Brian. So he wrote a poem. It made no difference that Gus was not exactly a candidate for poet laureate. All he cared about was writing from the heart and reaching out to his son with affirmation and encouragement.

Focus

Once we were riding in the car
I heard you speak of what you are
Then the thing that pleasured me
To hear your dream of what would be

Many rough and trying places
Seeing bloody, muddy faces
Wanting to get a chance to run
And find your own place in the sun

So you pressed on . . . to reach the mark
Discouraged oft'n with heavy heart
Steady creeping, stalking, lurking
Persevering, dreaming, working

And now you finally have your chance
To have your dream, you want to dance
So walk with God and be at peace
The golden ring's within your reach

And we who love you look with pride
At one who swam against the tide
Who chased his dream, and dared to dare
Who walked with God who brought him there

Gus folded the paper on which he had written his poem, and he smiled as he stuffed it in an envelope. After all, he was mailing it to the starting tight end of the Cleveland Browns.

Brian enjoyed the added responsibilities that came with being "the guy" when listening to his coaches game-plan for the tight end. He knew that being a starter brought added respect from his teammates, which meant a lot to him. But the best thing was simply getting to do what he had always known he could do: perform with the first-string offense. He was realistic enough to know that Belichick did not all of a sudden view him as a long-term solution to Bavaro's departure. Brian had not magically grown bigger or become faster at the age of twenty-eight. Then again, no NFL coach was in the business of handing out jobs to men who were not capable of performing. Why not take the opportunity and make the most of it?

After making only two receptions in his first five years in the NFL, Brian caught twenty-nine passes for an average gain of twelve yards in 1993. He also scored his first two touchdowns as a professional. He was never going to dazzle the defense by racing down the field and hauling in a game-changing bomb. But Brian was solid and dependable, a sure-handed receiver and—especially given his lack of size for a tight end—a remarkably rugged and efficient blocker. Brian also kept snapping, but with the addition of what he saw as a "monumental" benefit derived from being a regular player on offense. In earlier years, when he had to just stand on the sideline and wait to see what the offense would do, which would then dictate when he had to charge onto the field and snap, there was way too much time to think about all the negative possibilities and potential ramifications of his job. And—as if the mind games were not enough—he also routinely faced the physical challenge of entering a game cold for only one play at a time. Now that he was regularly playing offense, Brian no longer found himself standing around and getting stressed about snapping. When it came time for a punt or a kick, he simply broke from the huddle and went to the ball instead of lining up at tight end. It was just another play. He was already warm and into the flow of the game. As a result, he was more comfortable than ever with snapping—and his performance showed it. As stated in a summary of his season prepared by the Browns, Brian "served almost flawlessly as deep snapper."

The summary could have also said that Brian had continued his education in the Business of Professional Football 101, because 1993 was defined not only as a season of personal breakthrough for him, but also as a time of break-*up* between the Browns and one of Cleveland's all-time favorite athletes. It was the year that Belichick abruptly dumped quarterback Bernie Kosar, angrily releasing him from the team after a dustup in the middle of the season (it was not their first clash) and replacing him with Vinny Testaverde, a former Heisman Trophy winner who had joined the Browns after six years with the Tampa Bay Buccaneers. Cleveland fans were furious not only with the outright dismissal of Kosar, but also with Belichick's seemingly cold and detached handling of the situation. It did not help Belichick's cause when the Browns proceeded to lose six of eight games to close out their third-straight losing season. The Cleveland Stadium chants of "Bill must go" were silenced only by the completion of the schedule. Bill Belichick was not a popular man—not with the fans, not with the local media, not with his own players. He did not go, however, not then anyway—and neither did his tight end.

The next two years brought additional time as a starter for Brian—with totals of twenty-three starts and forty-four receptions in 1994 and 1995—along with even-more-dramatic twists and turns for the team as a whole. In a stunning reversal, the 1994 Browns went to the playoffs (Brian's first time playing in the post-season) with a record of 11–5. But then came another about-face: back to losing again, with an ugly mirror-image mark of 5–11 in 1995. That was not the worst of it. On November 6, 1995, with seven games left in the season, team owner Art Modell, struggling financially and unable to secure a deal for a new stadium in Cleveland, announced that he was going to move the franchise to Baltimore in 1996. The uproar in Ohio made the Kosar controversy look like minor-league stuff. But off went the Browns . . . soon to be renamed the Baltimore Ravens (and with Ted Marchibroda replacing Belichick as head coach).

The first-year Ravens were all about footballs flying in every direction. No team in the league gave up more passing yards than Baltimore's defense allowed. And only one team—the Jacksonville Jaguars— amassed more yards in the air than the Ravens did on offense. With Testaverde having the best year of his career at quarterback and top- notch wide receivers Michael Jackson and Derrick Alexander often drawing double coverages, Brian was perfectly positioned for the most productive season he would ever have. "I always knew Brian would be left in one-on-one coverage," Testaverde would later ex- plain. "Everyone would just put a linebacker or the strong safety on him, and before you knew it, Brian would be open by two steps. He was not a big-name guy. Never really had a lot of balls thrown to him before that. But fifty-five catches later, Brian has his career-year, and I have my career-year, too. Coincidence? I don't think so. We were very good friends, and we definitely helped each other a lot."

Marchibroda appreciated Brian for the same reasons Shula and

Belichick had: dependability, determination, intensity, work ethic, character, and intelligence. *Great guy to have on the ball club,* Marchibroda thought. Yet no matter how well Brian played in 1996, his coach still saw him as too small and too slow to be a permanent fixture at tight end. Marchibroda was always looking for someone a little better. And he eventually got the guy he wanted. When he told Brian that the Ravens were bringing in two-time Pro Bowl selection Eric Green, a former first-round draft pick of the Pittsburgh Steelers and one of the biggest tight ends in the NFL (six-foot-five, 280 pounds), Brian was devastated. He left Marchibroda's office with tears in his eyes, thinking, *If I'm not good enough to keep a starting job with the numbers I'm putting up, then I might as well just turn in my helmet and forget about it.* The hurt and the disappointment would never leave him, but Brian had never before quit on a group of teammates. Why start now? Lori kept encouraging him. She kept reminding him that being a starter was not the most important thing in the world: "Look at all the guys who never even get to play in the NFL, period—starter, second-string, special teams, whatever." And Brian ultimately stayed with the Ravens for two more years. That was a good thing for Matt Stover—for whom Brian had snapped ever since the day of that first game-winning field goal with the Browns back in 1991. With the help of Brian and a few different holders along the way, Stover became one of the most accurate field-goal kickers in NFL history. Although Brian's playing time on offense was greatly reduced by the arrival of Green, his contributions on special teams still made him a valuable commodity.

That was again evident soon after Marchibroda and his staff were fired following three straight losing seasons—1996 through 1998—in Baltimore. Special-teams coach Scott O'Brien, who had moved from Cleveland with the franchise and had now worked with Brian for eight years, quickly landed a job with the Carolina Panthers. His first assignment from head coach George Seifert was to find a new long snapper. *No-brainer,* as far as O'Brien was concerned. *Brian is a free agent. We just bring him in and get him signed.* And the Panthers did.

Nobody was more pleased with the acquisition than John Kasay, a Pro Bowl kicker who was entering his ninth season in the NFL. Kasay had never before worked with a snapper who was such a consummate professional, so precise and meticulous about every element of his job. Brian always had to have his special gloves on—he was the first snapper Kasay had ever seen wearing gloves—because they gave him the same feel on the ball no matter what the weather conditions. His feet always had to be the exact same distance apart when he was getting in his stance. And he would consistently "snap laces"—meaning that the football would reach the holder rotated to the point where his top hand was on the laces—thereby allowing the holder to easily place the ball on the ground with them facing away from the kicker (which makes for a better kick). But the most amazing thing to Kasay was the way Brian could always tell, and the way he would immediately point it out, if Kasay and holder Ken Walter were setting up improperly for a field goal. "We could be two inches off, and Brian would know it," Kasay would recall. "That attention to detail . . . that was always very personal to him." As were the results. "Brian never had a bad snap," Kasay said. "Not in practice. Not in warm-up. Not in a game. I mean, *never.*"

After thirteen years in the NFL, Brian certainly knew that outward expressions of gratitude and sentimentality were seldom part of the farewell routine, and almost never for anyone but a major star. Still, the way things ended in Carolina seemed harsh to him. After damaging cartilage in his right knee early in training camp, Brian played through the 2000 season as best he could because that was what his coaches wanted him to do. Sure, there were times when he had to beg off an assignment. But that was all part of the plan that was discussed with him: Play through the pain as best you can, *when* you can. A surgeon will clean you up after the season. And then you'll be back in the mix next year.

It did not happen that way. On Friday, March 2, 2001, two months after Brian had his surgery, Scott O'Brien called to let him know that the Panthers had decided to go in a different direction. They did not want him back. They were done with him. "Hardest call I've ever made," O'Brien would later say. "I mean, the guy had been laying it all on the line for me for years." Five with the Cleveland Browns. Three with the Baltimore Ravens. Two with the Carolina Panthers. But Brian was thirty-five. His knee was a question mark. And the Panthers had decided to replace him with a younger model. Three days later, they would sign long snapper Jason Kyle, a free agent who had played the previous year with the San Francisco 49ers.

Brian was understandably upset about losing the Carolina job. But it was the bigger picture that really brought him down. The rest of the league was done with him, too. Or at least everything very much looked that way. What would he do for the rest of his life? Where would he find his affirmation in the "real world" that awaited him beyond the familiar performance-based environment of professional sports? Of course, Brian had no way of knowing that the New England Patriots would eventually offer him one final glimpse of life in the NFL—a second chance that he never could have seen coming.

Six

One of the strangest things about being out of football was the recurring dream he kept having in the dead of night. In the beginning it came to him only once in a while. Then the frequency increased. There were variations. But the primary sequence was always pretty much the same: Brian would walk into the meeting room of an NFL team, all the sights and sounds so vivid, so real, and he would feel a wave of panic. Because nobody in the room knew who he was. Everybody stared at him and wondered what he was doing there. He felt like a new student showing up for the first day of class at a school where all the other kids already knew everybody. Where should he sit? What should he do? What should he say? Once the anxiety of the dream yielded to the reality of being awake, Brian usually required a few minutes to pack away the feelings of insecurity, to convince himself that he was actually forever done with football and would never have to face what he had just experienced with his eyes closed.

He was wrong about that. On the morning of Wednesday, December 17, 2003, his first official day of work as a member of the New England Patriots, Brian could not help but think of the dream that was so familiar to him. In fact, walking into his first team meeting, he could hardly believe what he was doing. *Wow, this is that moment from the dream,* Brian thought. *How surreal is this?* And he felt just as awkward as he did when he was sleeping through the scene. Brian was extremely self-conscious as he nodded hello to teammates he did not know. Maybe all eyes were not actually on him, but he sure felt as if they were. The way Brian figured it, everyone in the place had to be wondering, "Who is *this* guy?" The meeting room was filled with black, theater-style seats. Brian was concerned about sitting in one that might belong to someone else. That would be a bad way to start. So he turned for help to one of the few players he had known for years—punter Ken Walter— and they sat together without anyone else really paying any attention to them.

Once everyone settled down, Bill Belichick started with a few brief announcements, including a matter-of-fact introduction: "We have a new member of the team. Say hello to Brian Kinchen." A few of the more colorful "characters" on the team had long before established a standard response to the introduction of a newcomer. They would welcome him with a chorus of uniform shout-outs: "New dude. New dude." The only time they altered their greeting was when the new player had already been around the NFL long enough to be considered a sage veteran. Brian's teammates might not have known exactly how old he was—thirty-eight—or that he had just become the oldest player on the team. But their modified words of welcome made it perfectly clear that they knew they were taking on an elder. "New old-dude," they called out. "New old-dude."

The new old-dude just smiled. And his eyes were wide open. Brian was not dreaming this time. He was indeed back in the NFL—back as part of the hottest team in the league.

The Patriots had come a long way in just a few months. Sure, it was easy to look at them now and see only glorious possibilities. They had league glamour boy Tom Brady—already the youngest quarterback ever to win a Super Bowl and drawing comparisons to Joe Montana, of all people—directing the offense with great confidence. They had a stingy defense loaded with solid veterans: Ted Washington and Richard Seymour on the line; Tedy Bruschi, Willie McGinest, and Mike Vrabel at linebacker; Rodney Harrison and Ty Law in the backfield. They had a head coach who could hardly be discussed without the media pundits somehow working the word *genius* into their analysis. But things did not look nearly as good back in early September.

Five days before the 2003 season opener, Belichick ended a contract dispute with co-captain Lawyer Milloy by releasing the star safety—a seven-year veteran and four-time Pro Bowler, one of the best-known and most productive members of the 2001 championship team. The Patriots had already generated a plethora of questions by following their first Super Bowl victory with a 9–7 record that failed to earn them a spot in the 2002 playoffs. Now this: a controversial personnel move causing turmoil in the locker room. Players were angry and confused. They did not want to lose such an important teammate. Plus, they were well aware that if Belichick could say good-bye to someone who had contributed as much as Milloy had, he could just as easily dump almost any of them. The cold reality of players coming and going, for financial or other reasons, was by no means anything new in the business of professional football. But the departure of Milloy triggered unwanted media attention and became a major distraction—all of which was only heightened when Milloy quickly signed with the Buffalo Bills, who happened to be the Patriots' first opponent of the season. Playing in front of a fired-up home crowd, the Bills pummeled the Patriots from start to finish. They intercepted Brady four times. Milloy made one of the interceptions himself and also had a sack of Brady. Final score: Bills 31, Patriots 0.

Clearly, the Patriots had some major regrouping ahead of them if they wanted to make something of their season. They responded with a solid victory, 31–10, on the road against the Philadelphia Eagles, and then they claimed their home opener with a 23–16 win over the New York Jets. But the Patriots still were not hitting on all cylinders. In the fourth week of the season, they were stunned by one of the weakest teams in the league, the Washington Redskins, who defeated them 20–17. At the end of September, the Patriots had a perfectly mediocre record of two wins and two losses, and questions were again flying. What was wrong with them? Was the Super Bowl victory a one-time fluke? Were Belichick, Brady & Company moving toward a repeat of the previous season, heading down a path of futility that would ultimately dead-end prior to the playoffs?

The Patriots did not panic. Belichick continued preaching about preparation and execution. He kept reminding his staff and players that all they could do, all they *had* to do, was stick together and take one game at a time. That was exactly what they did. Brady and his receivers started clicking with a short passing game that kept costly mistakes to a minimum. The defense stiffened, confusing opponents with a variety of coverages and displaying a remarkable knack for forcing turnovers at the most opportune times. The victories started piling up. They were not always pretty: The Patriots gained only twenty-nine yards in the first half against the New York Giants. They scored only nine points, and won by only six, against the struggling Cleveland Browns. They needed overtime before putting away both the Miami Dolphins and the lowly Houston Texans. As Belichick had long been known to proclaim, though, "A win is a win."

After their two-and-two start, the Patriots ran off seven consecutive wins leading up to the heavyweight matchup that everyone had been waiting to see. In one corner, Belichick, Brady, and the Patriots. In the other, Tony Dungy, Peyton Manning, and the Indianapolis Colts. The date had been circled on calendars for months: November 30 in Indianapolis and on national television. The teams had identical 9–2 records. But they were quite different. The Patriots were dominant on defense. The Colts were an offensive juggernaut. Unless things in the NFL were to change dramatically in the next month, the outcome of this game would be critical in seeding for the upcoming playoffs and would probably determine which team would get home-field advantage if the Patriots and Colts were to meet again during the post-season. There was one other factor to consider: pure pride. The Patriots and Colts had a long history. And they really didn't care a whole lot for each other.

That only added to the tension as the game turned into an epic back-and-forth thriller. The Patriots jumped all over the Colts in the first half and stretched their lead to 31–10 in the third quarter. Then the Colts stormed back with three Manning touchdown passes to tie the game at 31–31 in the fourth. And all of that was only prelude to the real drama. The Patriots went back in the lead with a thirteen-yard touchdown pass from Brady to Deion Branch. But the Colts were far from done. With less than four minutes remaining and a first down at the New England eleven-yard line, they had an excellent opportunity to pull even again, but ended up having to settle for a short field goal. That left the Patriots with a four-point cushion, 38–34, with only 3:27 to play, but their offense was unable to run out the clock. Indianapolis got the ball back just inside New England territory, and Manning went to work. Six plays later, the Colts had first-and-goal at the two-yard line with forty seconds left in the game. They could manage only a single yard on three plays, though, so the whole game came down to this: Fourth-and-goal at the one. Fourteen seconds on the clock. Manning handed off to star running back Edgerrin James . . . James looked to run up the middle . . . but outside linebacker Willie McGinest charged in off the edge and stuffed him for a loss of a yard. Game over. McGinest sprinted down the field in wild celebration—an enduring image that would long live with Patriot fans as one of the most enjoyable memories of the season. The heart-stopping finish marked the fourth time in six weeks that the Patriots had gone until either the final minute of regulation or into overtime before locking down victory. Their winning streak was now at eight. And the *Boston Globe* had a new name for them: the Palpitation Pats.

Unbeknownst to Brian, the Patriots' next game was significant not only for them—clinching first place in their division with a 12–0 win over the Miami Dolphins in snow-covered Gillette Stadium—but also for him. With five and a half minutes left in the game, Patriots long snapper Lonie Paxton went down with a knee injury while blocking on a punt. He limped to the sideline but was sent back on the field because a holding penalty meant that the Patriots had to punt again. The do-over was a less-than-pleasant experience for a guy who had just torn the anterior cruciate ligament in his right knee. But the twenty-five-year-old Paxton did what he had to do. Since joining the team as a rookie free agent in the spring of 2000, he had snapped for every punt, every extra point, and every field-goal attempt—more than five hundred snaps in all. Paxton had also achieved an absolute rarity for a snapper: he had become known for something other than botching a snap. It happened at the conclusion of another snow game, a nail-biter against the Oakland Raiders in the 2001 playoffs, right after the Patriots' Adam Vinatieri kicked the winning field goal in overtime. Paxton celebrated by lying on his back and making snow angels in the end zone. The video was played over and over on television, and Paxton became something of a folk hero in New England. Two weeks later, Vinatieri kicked the Patriots to their Super Bowl victory with a dramatic forty-eight-yard field goal that defeated the highly favored St. Louis Rams on the last play of the game. And Paxton went right back to his signature move—this time pretending to make snow angels on the indoor turf of the Superdome in New Orleans. Of course, neither his ability to snap under pressure nor the notoriety that came from his childlike playfulness could do anything for Paxton now. He was done for the season. The Patriots needed a new snapper. "Not the type of thing you want to go through in December," Belichick told reporters covering the team. "But we don't really have any choice."

Following a tryout to which Brian was not invited, the Patriots signed a guy named Sean McDermott, who had spent one season with the Tampa Bay Buccaneers and another with the Houston Texans. He had also snapped for the Miami Dolphins earlier in 2003 but was released after struggling with his aim. In his first outing with the Patriots, a December 14 home game against the Jacksonville Jaguars, McDermott snapped nine times (four punts, three extra points, and two field goals) without causing any problems. But he also suffered a shoulder injury. The victorious Patriots—now winners of a franchise-record ten games in a row—needed to find yet another replacement snapper.

Worlds away in Baton Rouge, Louisiana, Brian had no idea what had happened to Paxton. He had never even heard of McDermott. And he certainly was not paying any attention to the Sunday football games. His television was on only for updates on the big news of the weekend: American soldiers had finally captured former Iraqi dictator Saddam Hussein. More than anything else, though, this was a family day for the Kinchens. Brian and Lori's oldest son, Austin, was celebrating his fourteenth birthday. It was a day for cake and candles, and for being wrapped in the lazy comforts of home. Sharing the afternoon with his wife and all four of his sons—eleven-year-old Hunter, seven-year-old Logan, and four-year-old McKane, in addition to the birthday boy—Brian could not have been more content with his surroundings. Of course, all of that was about to be dramatically altered by a phone call. It was the next morning—Monday, December

15, 2003—that Brian would interrupt his class to take a call from his old friend Scott Pioli.

Next thing Brian knew, he was trying on a new helmet and shoulder pads, and the Patriots equipment manager was grabbing jersey number forty-six for him.

Once that first team meeting was done and Brian was back in the locker room, he immediately returned to the same pre-practice routine that had served him well for thirteen seasons in the NFL. So what if he had been out of the league for three years? Why change anything now? Brian always liked to preserve as much free time as he could before practice—waiting until the last possible minute to get into his gear and join his teammates on the field—but he was also quite particular about his preparation. *Efficient* was the word he would use for it. He checked his laundry bag to make sure it contained everything he would need: jock, socks, and a T-shirt to go under his shoulder pads. He went to the training room, loaded up on rolls of pre-wrap, stretch tape, and standard white athletic tape, and he neatly stacked the rolls in his locker. (Brian almost never used a trainer to tape his ankles. Why waste time and energy waiting in line for that? He would just do it himself.) He checked his new cleats to make sure they fit and then worked over the rear uppers to break them in as best he could. (They were always too stiff when new.) Brian also tried on a new pair of gloves and flexed his fingers to make sure he had just the right feel. (For years he'd been wearing skin-tight synthetic-leather gloves to protect his hands while blocking and to help with his grip while snapping.) As uncomfortable as Brian had been walking into the meeting room, there was something about being back in the locker room, something about being back in his ritualistic preparation mode, that relaxed him and made everything feel normal again.

He was also comforted by reconnecting with the half dozen guys—both staff members and players—whom he knew from when they were all in Cleveland with Belichick and Pioli. One of Belichick's closest confidants, Ernie Adams, now carried the title "football research director," a position that often left players and others wondering who he was and what exactly he did. Eric Mangini, first a public-relations intern and then a coaches' assistant with the Browns, now coached the Patriots' defensive backs. Pepper Johnson, a teammate of Brian's in Cleveland, had also become a coach, working with the inside linebackers. Then there were two defensive linemen from the Browns who were again playing for Belichick: Rick Lyle and Anthony Pleasant. Practicing in Cleveland back when Brian played tight end on offense, he and Pleasant often engaged in direct battle at the line of scrimmage. No matter how rough things got on the field, though, they always remained good friends. Finally, there was the most unlikely longtime acquaintance of all, punter Ken Walter, who had rescued Brian by sitting with him in his first team meeting with the Patriots. When Brian played for the Browns, Walter was a college student who worked as a ball boy in their summer training camps. By 1999, when Brian joined the Carolina Panthers, Walter had become a punter in the NFL . . . for the Panthers! Walter was also the holder for field goals and extra points. For two years, Brian threw snaps to someone he first knew as a kid responsible for hauling ball bags and handing out towels. And now they would again be working together. *Man, you just never know,* Brian thought as he scanned a team roster he was using as a reference tool.

His first practice with the Patriots was held in the same indoor facility, the "bubble," in which his tryout had been conducted the day before. This was not a day for full gear or hard hitting. The players wore sweatpants, shoulder pads, and helmets. With everyone milling about before the group stretching period, one of the many players Brian did not know—he was wearing number fifty-four—approached him and extended a hand.

"Hey, Brian," he said. "I'm Tedy Bruschi." Thirty years old and in his eighth season with the Patriots, Bruschi was a fan favorite in New England. He was an inside linebacker, a captain of the defense, and one of the most respected guys on the team.

"Nice to meet you," Brian said.

Bruschi told him he remembered seeing him play on television. He even recalled a specific play from an old game against the Pittsburgh Steelers. Brian was amazed that Bruschi—that anyone—would actually remember something so ancient. More than anything, though, Brian was impressed that Bruschi had intentionally made a point of being so friendly to a new arrival.

Soon after that, Brian turned to see Tom Brady moving toward him and reaching out to shake hands. Of course, being unable to identify Brady would have been virtually impossible by this point in his meteoric rise to fame. In 2000, Brady was only a sixth-round draft pick and became the Patriots' fourth-string quarterback. By early the next season, though, he had worked his way up to the number-two slot, behind longtime franchise quarterback Drew Bledsoe. Then Bledsoe was sidelined with a chest injury. In stepped Brady, and he never looked back, leading the Patriots to the NFL championship and staking permanent claim to the starting job.

Now twenty-six years old and every bit a bachelor, Brady was much more than just a football star. With blue eyes, cleft chin, a mega-watt smile, and a squeaky-clean image, he had nonchalantly transcended the mere trappings of sport and jetted into the rarefied air of a full-fledged celebrity. He dated models and movie stars. He was featured on the cover of *Sports Illustrated,* which declared him "The New Prince of the NFL." But that was not enough. He also joined Jennifer Aniston and Denzel Washington among *People* magazine's "50 Most Beautiful People" of 2002. Through it all, Brady stressed that he just wanted to be "one of the guys" on the Patriots, and teammates insisted that his humility and hard work allowed him to fit right in.

"How you doing?" Brady said to Brian. "Good to have you on board."

"Thanks," Brian said. "Good to be here."

They spoke only briefly. But Brian would always remember it. He had been a lot of places in the world of football, had been around a lot of big-time quarterbacks and other star players through the years, and the way Brady handled himself was immediately distinguishable from the airs and attitudes of so many others. *Nice guy,* Brian thought. *Very genuine and down-to-earth.*

Early in practice, when Brian and the other specialists had nothing they had to do on the field, he wandered over to Belichick for a little chitchat. Belichick stood at ease in front of a few tackling dummies. He was dressed in sweats, his pants hanging loosely and open at the ankle zippers, his sweatshirt one of those signature charcoal gray hoodies, "New England Patriots Equipment" across the chest, that anyone who ever watched football was accustomed to seeing Belichick wear. His right hand was tucked in the front pouch of the sweatshirt. His left hand was twirling a whistle on its string around his fingers. It was not just the way he looked, though. Brian sensed that everything about Belichick was much more relaxed than it had been back in the Cleveland days. *Is it just that I'm coming in new and have not already had to listen to him all season long, like all the other guys?* Brian wondered. *Or has he actually found a way to chill out a little?*

"I've been thinking about my size," Brian told Belichick at one point in their conversation. "You think I'm heavy enough?"

"No," Belichick said. "But if you get run over, we'll just bring in somebody else who can get the job done."

They both smiled. Belichick was only joking. Or at least Brian took it that way.

As much thought and energy as Brian had put into the emotional shock and awe of being back in the NFL, the most natural part of his day came when it was finally time to perform the job he was hired to do. First came "live" drills with the punt team. Brian was understandably a bit anxious before unleashing his first snap. How could he not be? Everyone in the building was waiting to see what the new guy could do. Brian threw a strike into the waiting hands of Ken Walter. And all in the world was good. *Thwack. Thwack. Thwack.* Had he really been out of the game for three years?

Brian felt just as good, maybe even better, when it came time to work with the field-goal unit. *Like riding a bike,* he told himself. *Doesn't matter how long it's been. You don't forget how. Just hop on and ride.* Or in this case: just keep throwing strikes.

By the time practice was over and Brian was back in the locker room, all kinds of messages were waiting for him on his voicemail, both back at home in Baton Rouge and on the cell phone he had with him. Word of his signing with the Patriots had traveled quickly. Naturally, he had calls from family, friends, and former teammates with whom he had always kept in touch. But he also had messages from a few people with whom he had not spoken in years, long-ago acquaintances who wanted to offer congratulations and encouragement. One of the messages was from a woman Brian and his wife had befriended in Baltimore. She had some sort of a connection at a car dealership in the Boston area and wanted to arrange for Brian to have the use of a vehicle, at no charge, while he was with the Patriots. *Funny,* Brian thought. *Nobody ever called about a free car when I started teaching.*

Brian enjoyed calling everyone back and sharing the improbable story of his return to the NFL. He really had nothing else to do anyway. By early evening he was alone in his new quarters at an extended-stay hotel, room 108 at the Residence Inn in Foxborough, so he just kicked back and yakked away. Brian had never before so mindlessly run up so many minutes on his cell phone; he was not exactly one of the great free-spenders in the world. But roaming charges be damned, he was simply caught up in all the excitement and never once thought about the hundreds of dollars he was spending on air time. Everyone wanted to know what his first day with the Patriots had been like. Brian went on and on about how nice everyone had been and how so many of the players, Brady included, had gone out of their way to welcome him and to make him feel comfortable.

"Great group of guys," Brian told his dad. "It's hard to really explain it, but it almost feels like a college-type environment in terms of the camaraderie and the way people seem to genuinely enjoy being around each other. No real attitudes. No me-me-me types. Just a bunch of guys who work hard and have a good time together. It's definitely a different feel than anywhere else I've ever been." And it was not only the players. Brian said it was the whole atmosphere of the place, the overall feel of pure professionalism throughout the entire organization, that really impressed him: "Everything from the food in the cafeteria to the way they handle everything in the locker room. I mean, first-class organization from top to bottom. It just seems so obvious that something special is going on here."

The last call of the day was to say good night to Lori and the boys. Everyone already missed him. Mostly, though, Lori was just happy to hear how well things had gone with the first day of practice. She also had a school update for Brian. She had given the final exam to his classes, had just finished grading the tests, and his students had done well.

Lori wanted to share one of the responses to the essay portion of the exam. The instructions were: "Write about one thing that you learned in Bible this year that really made you think, changed your thinking, or made you have questions."

Some of the students focused their essays on something specific about Jesus. Some wrote about Christianity in general. Others highlighted the importance of a specific Gospel story or even a particular biblical passage. It was all fairly generic. But one girl turned in a refreshingly unique essay. She discussed something that Brian had talked about many times throughout the fall: the fact that he was done with football and was teaching at Parkview because that was where God wanted him to be. "I'm confused," the girl wrote, "because now Mr. Kinchen is in New England playing for the Patriots. Does God want him here or does God want him there?"

Seven

It did not take Brian long to feel that he was exactly where he was supposed to be. His second day of practice, outside this time, gave him all the confidence he needed. The wind was howling, blowing in all directions, and with no pattern or predictability. Yet when it came time for the special teams to go through their repetitions, Brian could not have been more pleased with the accuracy of his snaps. One of the reasons Belichick and Pioli had signed him was that, thanks to his years in Cleveland, Brian came to them with a lot of experience playing in bad weather. He was very good at blocking out all external factors beyond his control and simply focusing on mechanics, and now he was performing with the ease and comfort of a dependable veteran.

Thwack. Thwack. Thwack. Brian kept firing strikes through the chilly December air. He was not doing anything out of the ordinary. He was just doing his job without being noticed. Wind? What wind? The more snaps he threw, the less he had to wonder whether he really belonged back in the NFL. Brian even went so far as to imagine his coaches thinking: *How in the world has this guy been out of the league for so long?*

His confidence soaring, Brian wanted to contribute however he could. He was not foolish enough to think that Belichick or any other coach in his right mind would have any interest in the services, even as a reserve player, of a thirty-eight-year-old tight end who was underweight and had not run a pass route in three years. But what about stepping in with the offensive scout team and helping to give the first-string defense a good look at plays the New York Jets would probably be running against the Patriots that weekend? Brian had never wanted to be one of those single-duty snappers who just sat off to the side with the punter and kicker while everyone else was going at it during practice. He never wanted to be one of those specialists that other guys on the team would tease about their lack of activity. Plus, spending so much time on the sideline, just watching, made him feel worthless. So he went to Belichick and asked if it would be okay for him to run some plays with the scout team.

"Whatever you want to do, but you better not get hurt," Belichick replied evenly. "You better make sure you're able to do the job we hired you to do."

It was during the final practice of his first week that Brian, kneeling on the sideline along with punter Ken Walter and kicker Adam Vinatieri, decided to make his move into the offensive huddle.

"I'm gonna go see about running some routes," Brian matter-of-factly announced while rising to his feet.

"What?" said an incredulous Walter.

"Yeah, just a few," Brian said.

Walter and Vinatieri neither encouraged nor discouraged him. They just stayed right where they were, in full relaxation mode, and readied themselves for what figured to be an amusing interlude that would break up the monotony of watching yet another set of practice plays for the umpteenth time.

Brian walked slowly toward the center of the field, where Ivan Fears, an assistant coach in charge of running backs, was flashing diagrams of Jets plays for the scout team to mimic. *Do I really want to do this?* Brian asked himself. *Am I really being smart here?* He contemplated what Belichick had told him about getting hurt. After all, the Patriots had already lost two snappers in the previous two weeks. He also thought about the fact that he had not run a pass route in years, and he reminded himself of the uniquely strenuous demands placed on the legs of a hard-charging receiver, especially when going full speed and coming out of a break, which requires planting a foot and then immediately pushing off in a new direction. Brian stood behind the huddle and thought about all that while the offense ran a few more plays. Then he came to his senses. *Ah, forget it,* he told himself. Serving the team by staying healthy and being able to snap far outweighed any potential contribution of running a few routes with the offense. Brian turned away from the action, walked back to Walter and Vinatieri, and told them he had changed his mind.

"Smart move," Walter said.

"Don't know what you were even thinking about," Vinatieri added.

Aside from his aborted visit to the offensive huddle, every other facet of Brian's on-field return to professional football was about as simple and seamless as possible. But that did not mean that the overall experience of returning to the NFL came without its

challenges. The biggest was being so abruptly and completely up-
rooted from the daily rhythms and routines of a life with which
Brian had become quite comfortable. Simply put, he missed his
wife and children. He missed teaching and visiting with the kids
in his classes. He even thought about the LSU football team he
had been helping for two years as a volunteer assistant, first breaking down opponents' game films for head coach Nick Saban, then
working with the long snappers, punters, and kickers. What a time
to be gone. LSU was preparing to play Oklahoma in the national
championship game, the first shot at a national title for LSU since
Gus Kinchen and his teammates went undefeated back in 1958.

In addition to missing all that he had left behind in Louisiana,
Brian also had to adjust to the mundane realities of being in a setting
that was both new and temporary: living alone in a hotel room; relying on a teammate for rides to and from practice until that friend
from Baltimore could get him a car; learning his way around the
Boston suburb of Foxborough, home of the Patriots. Although his
room had a small kitchen area, he never went shopping for gro-
ceries. He just ate at the team facility or picked up something at a
restaurant or convenience store. Nobody had promised Brian that
the life of a short-term football mercenary would be glamorous. He
filled most of his downtime by watching television, reading a book,
or sitting on the edge of his bed talking on the telephone to family
and friends. He also set aside quiet time for prayer and attended a
weekly Bible study that linebacker Don Davis led for anyone on the
team who wanted to participate. More than anything else, though,
Brian simply waited. He waited for the glitz and glitter of the NFL
that truly shines only once a week. He waited for the unparalleled
rush of game day.

Saturday, December 20, 2003. East Rutherford, New Jersey. New England Patriots against the New York Jets in a nationally televised night game at the Meadowlands. The 12–2 Patriots would be trying to lock down home-field advantage throughout the upcoming play-offs. The 6–8 Jets had already been eliminated from any chance of post-season play but were nonetheless eager for a prime-time upset of their much-publicized division rival. As Jets quarterback Chad Pennington told reporters, "We might as well take somebody down with us." The excitable New York fans would be all for that. They were already certain to be fired up by a heavily promoted halftime event honoring the best players from all four decades of franchise history, which would mean a rare appearance by the most revered of all New York Jets, Hall of Fame quarterback Joe Namath. ESPN was also hyping the game—and itself—because the Patriots–Jets matchup was the cable network's two hundredth telecast of an NFL game. None of that mattered to Brian. All he wanted to do was get on and off the field without being noticed.

Players had different ways of greeting the tension of game day. Some got louder and more animated than usual. Others became withdrawn as their faces tightened with anticipation and purpose. Brian's way was to quietly rely on order and routine. Just as he had gone right back into his old ritualistic preparation prior to his first practice with the Patriots, Brian automatically returned to his standard procedures for the final hours leading up to a game.

After taking the last bus from the team hotel to the Meadow-lands, he spent his first few minutes in the locker room organizing his uniform, equipment, and tape just the way he would want them when it came time to ready himself for action. Then he took off all his clothes, wrapped a towel around his midsection, and walked across the room to claim a bathroom stall—and not only for standard activity. He also used the privacy of a stall to pray before a game. Brian did not pray for victory. He prayed for the ability to put forth his best efforts; for protection against the many ills that could so easily visit themselves upon anyone playing such a violent sport; and for the strength to be prepared for whatever might happen out on the field, no matter what the circumstances of a given play or the eventual outcome of the game. When he was done praying, Brian took a hot shower, steaming hot. Physically, it helped him get loose. Mentally, it also helped to relax him. Then he hunkered down on a stool in front of his locker and casually flipped through the pages of a game program (the same souvenir magazine sold throughout the stadium). Brian was always curious to see if there were any familiar faces on the other team. In this case, he already knew that he would be playing against two longtime friends. Vinny Testaverde, a former teammate with the Cleveland Browns and Baltimore Ravens, was now the second-string quarterback for the Jets. Mike Westhoff, his first special-teams coach with the Miami Dolphins, was now in the same role with the Jets. Brian looked forward to seeing them both. For now, though, with a clock on the wall showing 7:10, it was time to get dressed for the game. Brian and his fellow specialists were due on the field to begin warm-ups in twenty minutes. The game would start at 8:30.

How many times through the years had Brian made a similar walk from the sheltered cocoon of a locker room out to a field of play on which dreams would both flourish and flop in full view of sports fans across the nation? Yet this time was different than ever before. Brian would have denied that with the nonchalance of a seasoned professional: "Only doing what I've always done." But this was no longer the same as it had always been for him. Never before had three years passed between games. Never before had he taken one giant step from a seventh-grade classroom to a top-tier NFL team. Brian wondered what it would feel like to run onto the field the first time he was needed in the game: *What's it going to be—a punt, a field goal, an extra point?* And then there was this: *How will it go? How will I do?* Warm-ups went perfectly well. But as the Patriots and Jets lined up for Adam Vinatieri's opening kickoff, Brian was not his usual self on the sideline. He was uncharacteristically anxious. All he could think about was getting on the field and getting his first snap out of the way.

As things turned out, the beginning of the game could not have been scripted any better for him. On the second play from scrimmage, linebacker Tedy Bruschi intercepted a Chad Pennington pass, giving New England the football at the New York thirty-five-yard line. Tom Brady took the field and immediately threw a touchdown pass to wide receiver David Givens. Only forty-eight seconds into the game, it was time for Brian to go to work. He pulled on his helmet, grabbed his mouthpiece, which he kept tucked under his belt, and ran onto the field for the extra point. Brian had done it so many times that it was an almost mindless experience for him. All he was doing was getting on a bike again.

His snap to Ken Walter was right where they wanted it, and the hold was equally uneventful. Vinatieri put boot to ball . . . and the extra point was perfect. Brian returned to the sideline without anyone needing to know who he was. Life was good.

The rest of the game went just as well for both Brian and the Patriots. Brian ended up snapping the ball nine times (six on punts and three on extra points) without incident. The Patriots intercepted

Pennington four more times after that initial pick-off and—with a final score of 21–16—extended their winning streak to eleven games. As was often the case with the Patriots, there was nothing particularly flashy or memorable about the way they played. It was strictly business as usual.

In fact, the most widely talked about "highlight" of the ESPN broadcast had nothing to do with the game itself. Late in the second quarter, sideline reporter Suzy Kolber interviewed Joe Namath, who had clearly enjoyed more than a splash of liquid refreshment in advance of the halftime ceremony. Almost thirty-five years after Namath had first guaranteed and then delivered victory over the heavily favored Baltimore Colts in Super Bowl III, Kolber asked the sixty-year-old "Broadway Joe" what it meant to him that the Jets had been struggling. Leaning in toward the stunned reporter, who was young enough to be his daughter, Namath said, "I want to kiss you. I couldn't care less about the team struggling." And then—as if Kolber or any football-watching fan in America possibly could have missed it the first time—Namath once again offered up his desire to kiss her. His alcohol-enhanced performance would quickly take on a celebrity-gossip life of its own, and Namath would soon issue a public apology. No doubt about it, there are times when even the most legendary of football heroes would not mind borrowing—if only temporarily—the no-name, no-attention existence of a long snapper.

Eight

For a family with four generations of roots firmly planted in South Louisiana, the likelihood of a last-minute Christmas gathering in a suburb of Boston was highly improbable, and the logistics were hardly conducive to any grand festivities. Brian met Lori and their four boys at Logan Airport in the middle of the afternoon. His parents, unable to get on the same flights as everyone else, did not arrive until late in the evening, but they didn't miss much. Christmas dinner was devoid of any ceremony or celebration. Lori just threw together a hodgepodge of whatever she could find at the hotel, primarily sandwiches and snacks Brian had picked up earlier, and the Kinchens hunkered down in Brian's room.

The only visual clue announcing the existence of a special occasion was a little fake Christmas tree, all of three feet tall, that Brian had adorned with minimal lighting and relegated to an out-of-the-way spot on a counter in the kitchen area. No boxes of any heft could have possibly fit under it, but the boys had already opened gifts at home in Louisiana. Brian had not done much shopping in Foxborough. He gave Lori a curling iron; she could only conclude that he simply wanted to have *something* for her. And he told the boys that their weeklong visit—which would include going to the Patriots game on Saturday—was a Christmas gift. They would also get to pick whatever team gear they wanted once they could get in the Patriots Pro Shop and look around after the holiday.

The Saturday-afternoon game against the Buffalo Bills marked the end of the regular season for New England. Nobody associated with the Patriots had forgotten what the Bills had done to them in the season opener (blowing them out by a score of 31–0 and raising legitimate concerns about what was left to come in 2003). With the fortunes of the two teams now dramatically reversed, the Patriots rolling with a 13–2 record and the struggling Bills arriving in Foxborough at 6–9, fans in New England were fired up about the opportunity for a redemption game. With that in mind, and with home-field advantage throughout the playoffs not yet clinched, the Patriots got right down to business, scoring four unanswered touchdowns in the first half. The final score even came in perfectly symmetrical form—31–0 again—this time with the Patriots blanking the Bills. Their twelfth straight victory meant they would march into the playoffs with the best record in the league.

Much of the post-game attention rightly focused on the dominant defense the Patriots had been playing for quite some time, and especially at home. In their last six games at Gillette Stadium, the Patriots had allowed only one touchdown and a total of a measly twenty-two points. Three of those games had been shutouts. But at least one family among the 68,436 people in attendance for the Patriots–Bills game was focused on something other than defensive statistics. As excited as the Kinchens were about everything else going on with the Patriots, only one set of numbers was critical to them: nine snaps for Brian in the season finale—four on extra points, three on punts, two on field-goal attempts—with zero reason for anyone else to ever think or talk about any of them. *Business as usual,* Brian told himself. In fact, the only thing out of the ordinary for him was the post-game celebration on the field. He had never before been part of an NFL team that had so much to be genuinely excited about. But there was also the reality of being so new to the Patriots. How involved could he really feel in all the revelry? Brian walked slowly off the field, intentionally taking time to look around and soak up the atmosphere, and enjoying the wonderful energy. He also felt somewhat strange, however—still a bit of an outsider looking in.

In the stands, Lori had run into Bill Belichick's wife, Debby, whom she knew from Cleveland. They had hugged and exchanged family updates. And now Debby took Lori to her husband's office so that Lori could say hello once he was done with his players and the media. "Surprise!" Lori said when the coach finally entered. After greetings and a few minutes of chitchat, Lori sincerely thanked Belichick for calling Brian and for giving them the opportunity to hop on the Patriots' bandwagon. "It's so great to be here," Lori said. "I mean, I can't even tell you how much fun this has already been for all of us."

The Patriots had indeed earned both home-field advantage throughout the playoffs and a bye in the first week. With Belichick apparently feeling the holiday spirit, he began 2004 by giving players and staff a long weekend off, from New Year's Day through Sunday, January 4. That enabled Brian to fly back with his family for a few days in Baton Rouge. After being gone for almost three weeks, he was excited to be home. With Parkview closed for the holidays, Brian would not see his students. But he did bring a box of small gifts for them—a generous supply of Patriots trinkets, including team photos, stickers, and fanny packs. Lori would distribute them in school on Monday. Brian also taped a video message for Lori to play in his classes.

Sitting in his home office Saturday night, wearing a red T-shirt and a white Patriots cap, Brian stared into a camera he had set up on his desk and created a tape with all the production value of a hostage video. The camera tightly framed him from chest up, with the top of his head not quite making it into the picture, his face unintentionally darkened by shadows. And the tone of Brian's delivery was not exactly scintillating. But this was not about quality of presentation. It was only about letting his students know that they were still in his thoughts. Brian started by asking them to take out their notebooks because he wanted to give them one more lesson and then one more test. "Just joking," he quickly assured them. With the semester ending, making this the last time Brian would address these kids as his students, what he really wanted to do was speak from the heart.

"I love each and every one of you, and have enjoyed being around you," Brian said. "Some have pushed me, and tested me, and taken advantage of my kindness. Others have been perfect angels. And, obviously, a lot of you are in between. But I have enjoyed each and every one of you."

Brian said he would be back "in a month or so"—which would mean making it all the way to the Super Bowl. He told his students about the goodies that "Miss Lori" would be handing out to them. Then he asked his students for their prayers and support, told them that he prayed for all of them each day, and closed with this: "I hope that you continue in your walk with the Lord. Hopefully . . . God has used me to help you in your walk and strengthen you in your faith. And that's about all. Wish I had more to say. I know it's probably kind of boring, and you probably want to get to the playground, or something like that. But I love you and miss you, and I'll see you soon. Thanks."

The next night, Sunday the fourth, was the game Louisiana football fans had been waiting for, *hoping* for, all season. Actually, they had been waiting and hoping for much longer than that—ever since LSU won its first national championship in 1958. Even the location of the big game was a gift for LSU fans. The Sugar Bowl matchup between top-ranked Oklahoma and second-ranked LSU—which also carried the distinction of being the Bowl Championship Series national title game—would be played in New Orleans, in the Tiger-friendly confines of the Louisiana Superdome.

What a temptation for Brian. He was only seventy miles away in Baton Rouge. LSU coach Nick Saban had already called him with two tickets to the game—a gesture of thanks for his volunteer work throughout the year. But Brian had to be back with the Patriots the next morning. He found an early-Monday flight out of

New Orleans that was scheduled to get him back to Boston in time. But what if he encountered a flight delay or cancellation? He could not afford to take that chance. Plus, he really wanted Austin and Hunter to get the enjoyment of seeing the game in person. Brian's dad and brother Todd were already going. Now they could take Brian's two oldest boys with them.

With that settled, Brian left Baton Rouge early enough Sunday to be back in his Foxborough hotel room in time to watch LSU on television. It was stressful enough to watch from afar as a team he cared so much about—had spent so much time helping—was battling such a strong opponent for the glory of being number one. A personal subtext further heightened the drama. Steve Damen, LSU's regular snapper for punts and therefore one of the players with whom Brian had worked the most, had been suspended for selling his complimentary tickets to the game (a violation of the amateur rules governing collegiate athletics). Gant Petty, another player with whom Brian had regularly worked, would have to fill in. Petty had already been snapping for field goals and extra points, but he had never snapped for a punt in a game. Now he faced the daunting challenge of his first chance coming in the bright spotlight of the national championship game. The less-than-ideal circumstances left Brian on edge.

Things went well for LSU. Amazingly enough, though, with only nine seconds left in the game, and with Petty having done absolutely fine up to that point, LSU still needed one more clean effort by the punt team to secure victory. The Tigers were ahead 21–14. On fourth down, they had the ball on their own forty-eight-yard line. Out came the punt team. One bad snap, and Oklahoma could possibly pull off a miracle win. One good operation from the punt team, and LSU would give the state of Louisiana its first national title in forty-five years—in other words, sheer euphoria. Punter Donnie Jones looked downfield and saw that Oklahoma was setting up without a return man. He knew that the Sooners would be "bringing the house"—rushing him with everyone they had and trying to block the punt.

"Come on, Gant, just put it in his hands," Brian told the television in his hotel room.

Petty snapped the ball perfectly. Jones caught it with no problem, quickly turned the ball so its laces were up, and kicked it away. By the time the ball rolled out of bounds at the Oklahoma twelve-yard line, all nine of those seconds had expired and the LSU Tigers were national champions.

"Yes!" Brian shouted.

Watching the wild celebration in the Superdome, he knew that Austin and Hunter had to be having the time of their lives. Sure, he would have enjoyed sharing the moment with them and everyone else back in Louisiana. But at least he knew he would be on time for work the next morning. And Brian also knew he would have bragging rights—"Number one, baby! LSU is back on top!"—in the Patriots' locker room.

LSU fans all over Louisiana were caught up in Tigermania the next morning, especially in Baton Rouge, where offices and schools were filled with many more smiling faces than would normally be found early on a Monday. Parkview was no exception, and the level of excitement in Brian's classes only increased when Lori opened the box of Patriots paraphernalia and handed out the gifts he had gathered for his students. Patriots stickers were soon affixed not only to notebooks and clothing, but also to the cheeks and fore-heads of a few kids. Fanny packs were creatively placed—a boy named A.C. Turner wrapped one around his head—to make a variety of fashion statements. And the girls wasted little time before examining the team photos to pick out their teacher's hottest team-mates. (Tom Brady was no surprise as the consensus favorite, but linebacker Mike Vrabel and tight end Christian Fauria also drew a considerable amount of attention and even a few shrieks from the twelve- and thirteen-year-olds.)

Lori did well to get everyone settled down long enough to show the video Brian had made. The students enjoyed seeing him. But they liked it even more when Lori told them she had a video camera with her and suggested making their own tape to send Brian. Slowly panning the classroom, Lori told Brian, "Here's your wonderful class. They miss you so much." Then she asked the students if they had any "words of wisdom" for him. They did not respond with much that could be construed as wisdom, but they did do a lot of smiling and laughing and waving, and they offered a wonderful collection of enthusiastic shout-outs that would later fill their teacher with pride and joy.

"We love you, Mr. Kinchen."

"Good luck with the Patriot people."

"Your video wasn't boring. Your video was *cool*."

"My birthday's coming up. I'll see you when I'm thirteen."

"We miss you. Peace out!"

The unmistakable showstopper was a scripted performance led by Ashley Thornton, one of the girls who three weeks earlier had tried with such determination to catch one of Brian's snaps on the playground before he first left for Boston. Ashley now stood between classmates Rachel Jackson and Meagan Breaux, the three of them side-by-side, with brand-new fanny packs wrapped around their waists. On cue, they looked into the camera with ear-to-ear smiles and spoke in unison: "Tom Brady, you're a cutie! Don't worry, Mr. Brian, you're a cutie, too!"

Lori later invited a smattering of Parkview teachers and administrators to be part of her video as well. Some were entirely kind and sincere—sending good wishes for Brian and his teammates. Others hit Brian up with semi-serious requests for Patriots T-shirts and tickets to a game. More than anything, though, his colleagues offered silly banter and friendly jabs.

Eighth-grade Bible teacher Sonya Pruitt held up a newspaper story in which Brian had been quoted as saying that he had just been "chilling" with his students when he got the call from the Patriots—and she teased him about his word choice. "When have you started using the word *chilling*?" Pruitt asked, big smile lighting up her face. "And just for the record, if you're trying to be cool, *chilling* is way out. So you gotta get with it and pick a new word."

In one of the most creative scenes, Dairon Bueche, who taught Louisiana history to eighth graders and was also a baseball coach, made light of Brian's job with the Patriots by lining up in a school hallway to snap an apple to Brad Duffy, who was both a teacher and the middle school athletic director. Duffy stood behind Bueche in the role of a punter.

"We were wondering," Bueche said before getting down in position over his apple, "you're making what, like thirty, forty thousand dollars a week now—just how hard *is* your job? I mean, look . . . I think I can do this."

While snapping his apple, though, Bueche was caught off guard by another teacher, Alisha Stutzman, a smiley, energetic blonde, who playfully rushed him and pushed him back the way a defensive lineman would. The apple bounced on the floor before Duffy could get to it, prompting an immediate personnel move.

"You're fired," Duffy informed Bueche. "You're cut."

Ah, the loyalty and respect that come with being employed as a long snapper.

Even the school principal, Cooper Pope, who had been fully supportive when Brian pondered whether he should go to the New England tryout and had been openly congratulatory when he actually signed with the Patriots, now got into the act with an impressive flair for both fiction and taunting. It helped that the forty-year-old Pope was himself a football guy, having been an offensive lineman at Mississippi College and now coaching at Parkview. Standing in the teachers' lounge, his left arm leaning against a soft-drink vending machine, Pope started his performance for the camera by telling Brian he had watched him on television and thought he had snapped real well. "But I noticed that even the punter got down the field before you did," Pope said with mock seriousness, successfully fighting off a smile for the time being. "I'm not saying you're out of shape, or you've lost your speed . . . or maybe somebody blocked you straight to the ground. I'm not sure what happened. But, uh, just a little concerned. I was gonna call Belichick and maybe see if we could work on some plyometrics, or some explosion drills, to get you to snap and *explode* off the ball, and avoid that block, and get down the field." Pope could no longer control himself. He finally let loose with a burst of laughter. "Is that good enough?" he asked Lori.

Oh, yes, the principal's performance was definitely good enough. No question, Brian would be hitting the rewind and play buttons more than once.

Alone with his thoughts in Massachusetts, Brian was keenly aware that he was in the midst of something both unique and magical. He certainly could not cite any other example of a Bible teacher being called out of class to play for the hottest team in the NFL. After three years away from the league, it was shocking enough that a thirty-eight-year-old former journeyman would be called out of retirement by *any* team, no matter *what* he was doing at the time. But that was only the beginning. There was also the bonus— enhanced by Lori being his substitute teacher—of his ability to stay so connected with the kids back at Parkview while this seemingly made-for-Hollywood tale continued to unfold. Clearly, the excitement at school was building with the Patriots about to host their first playoff game against the Tennessee Titans. And then there was even the remarkable timing of what the LSU Tigers had just done—the team Brian had been helping for two years going on to win the national championship while he was away getting ready for the NFL playoffs.

In his wildest dreams, Brian never could have conjured up such a far-fetched confluence of events. And so he finally started doing something he had been thinking about for a while. Sitting at the desk in his hotel room the evening of Thursday, January 8, two days before the game against the Titans, he pulled out a tape recorder—a small handheld recorder made for microcassettes— that he had recently purchased specifically for this. And he hit the record button. How else could he possibly document this incredible journey he was living? How else could he possibly freeze this time with the Patriots and store it away so that he could later pass it down through his family? A friend had suggested that he start writing a diary, but Brian knew he would never keep up with that, and he figured that an "audio journal" would serve the same purpose. So he started talking into his little recorder. The first words he spoke, so simple and straightforward, had nonetheless been utterly unimaginable only twenty-four days earlier: "I am in Foxborough, Massachusetts. I have joined the New England Patriots . . ."

Brian gave brief summaries of some key events he had already experienced: the initial call from Pioli during class; the trip to Boston and the tryout; signing with his new team and playing in those last two games of the regular season. He said he was "very pleased" with his performance so far, especially considering that so much time had passed during which he hadn't taken any snaps—during which he hadn't even *thought* about throwing any footballs between his legs. Brian talked about the way everyone with the Patriots had been so welcoming. And he mentioned the Bible-study sessions he'd been attending with teammates. Brian had quickly developed a good friendship with the leader of the sessions, Don Davis, a linebacker in his first year with the Patriots and eighth in the NFL. The friendship started because of their shared spirituality, but it grew because Brian and Davis really enjoyed each other. Their conversations were open and genuine—and Brian saw his new friend as yet another reason to be grateful for his temporary place in New England. "Life here has been good," he said. "I am just so thankful the Lord has put me here."

Nine

When Lori went back to Foxborough for the Patriots' divisional playoff game against the Tennessee Titans, she traveled not only as a wife and mother—taking Austin and Hunter and a friend of each with her—but also as a delivery service. She had the students' video to give Brian, and they had also created an impressive collection of cards and letters for him. They were variously addressed with quite a trio of honorifics for a professional football player: "Mister," "Coach," and "Professor." Some of the cards and letters were adorned with football drawings that were both colorful and primitive. All the missives included Bible verses and personal messages.

The juxtaposition of the two sometimes made for especially rich reading. Sean O'Neal began with his own take on Psalm 16:3: "The godly people in our land are my true heroes! I take pleasure in them!" Then, right below that, he wrote: "I hope you do great! Kick some booty in the playoffs." Brian was all for that. First, though, sitting in his hotel room on Friday, January 9, the night before the game, he wanted to read the rest of his "mail" and see what else he might find.

Each message brought its own joy. One thing was quickly apparent: the seventh graders of Parkview Baptist were big on exclamation points.

"You're the BOMB!!"

"Don't come back till you win!"

"I have been watching you on T.V. but all I manage to see is youre Butt!"

The spelling and punctuation were not always perfect. But the tone and energy were.

From Matt Nicols: "you can do all things through christ who strengthens me. as in get to the super bowl."

From Kristi: "you are the best teacher! I hope yall make it to the bowls or whatever they are."

From Robert Vaughn: "When you snap the ball wave when the play is over."

From Clay: "I think that you need to get fatter. Only 5 more Big Macs and a few more workouts."

From Wesley Perkins, the boy who had done such a good job catching snaps for Brian the day he took that one class outside before heading to Boston for his tryout: "My first pick was the chiefs but how can you pull against your own Bible teacher . . . Go Pats"

Of course, a few of the girls could not help but include the obligatory Tom Brady references.

From Ashley Thornton: "Oh Mr. Tom Brady your so fine! Im the girl on the video with blonde hair! By the way any single NFL players you can give me a call! (hint hint Tom Brady)"

As much as Brian was amused by such silliness, it was the sincerity of one letter, one of the longest and most heartfelt in the whole pile, that really made him pause to think about and cherish his relationships with his students. "We miss you so much!" Jennie Garland began, "but that's not the point." No, with the semester winding down, meaning that she would no longer be in class with "Mr. Brian" (as she called him), Jennie wanted him to know how important he was to her. "You are a blessing," she wrote. "You know just what to say and when & how to say it. No teacher . . . can top that." Using her own form of punctuation, Jennie spelled out the greatest lesson she had learned in class: "*If you believe something with all your heart, you can make it happen*" Then she wrote: "you really made me appreciate something I learned in school . . . that's a first, seriously. I just wanted to let you know how much you mean to me. I'm really glad that you came to teach! I will miss you so much next semester! I'm going to say hey in the halls! LOL! I ❤ U so much . . . thanks for bein you! You are an angel in a football body, whether you believe it, or not, I do. Thank you so very, very, very much for making such an impact on my life!"

When he was done reading, Brian was still sitting at the foot of his hotel bed. Yet he was also floating off somewhere he had never before been—reflecting on a profound and unexpected payoff from his first semester at Parkview. When he became a teacher, Brian was doing it because he wanted to influence the lives of young people. Now he was the one who felt like the true beneficiary of that process. He had certainly never experienced any such feeling of fulfillment from anything he had ever done—from anything he had ever accomplished—in the world of sports.

The warmth Brian felt from reading those cards and letters was soon replaced by the bone-chilling harshness of a frigid day, Saturday, January 10, in New England. Playing at night only made it more uncomfortable at Gillette Stadium, where the temperature would be four degrees with a wind chill of minus ten at the start of the Patriots–Titans game (the coldest game in the history of either team). Jim Nantz of CBS opened the national television broadcast by telling viewers they were looking live at "the frozen tundra of Foxborough." Fans had been given special permission to bring blankets and sleeping bags into the stadium, and players had been "outfitted with a whole host of arctic weather gear," Nantz noted. Tennessee coach Jeff Fisher said that handling the ball would be an issue. "What you got to look for is the snappers, and the holders, and the kicking game, and protecting the football," he told sideline reporter Armen Keteyian. "But . . . I don't think any team's got an advantage over the other."

The Patriots and the Titans—led by NFL co-MVP Steve McNair at quarterback, four-time Pro Bowl selection Eddie George at running back, and sack specialist Jevon "The Freak" Kearse at defensive end—had already shown that they were pretty evenly matched. In the fifth game of the season, on October 5, New England had outlasted Tennessee, 38–30, in a back-and-forth game that was not decided until the Patriots scored two touchdowns late in the fourth quarter. It was the victory that started the Patriots' winning streak. More than three months later, McNair (strained right calf and sprained left ankle) and George (dislocated left shoulder) were now dinged up after a physical opening-round playoff game against the Baltimore Ravens. But this was no time to worry about aches and pains. The Patriots were 14–2, the Titans 13–4. The winner of this game would be only one more victory away from the Super Bowl. The loser would be done for the year.

On their first possession, the Patriots opened the scoring with a forty-one-yard touchdown pass from Brady to rookie wide receiver Bethel Johnson. The Titans answered quickly by driving sixty-one yards and evening the score, 7–7, on a five-yard touchdown run by Chris Brown. Then, early in the second quarter, the Patriots regained the lead, 14–7, when Antowain Smith capped an eleven-play drive with a one-yard touchdown run through the left side of the line.

For the Patriots' Bible-teacher-turned-long-snapper, all of that was merely preamble for the personal drama that was soon to unfold. After stalled drives by both Tennessee and New England, 5:35 remained in the second quarter when the Patriots lined up on their own thirty-seven-yard line for their first punt of the game. Brian had already thrown three perfectly good snaps—two on extra points after the touchdowns and one on a forty-four-yard field-goal attempt that Adam Vinatieri had missed wide to the left. The primary thought now on Brian's mind was something technical he'd been working on in practice: keeping his hips locked down throughout his punt snaps so that the ball would not sail too high. He had thrown a few high balls in practice that week, but he believed he had solved the problem by slightly adjusting his mechanics. Now, on fourth-and-five against the Titans, Brian positioned himself over the football with the same ease and comfort that had always served him so well through the years. *Hips down,* he reminded himself one last time. He gripped the ball with his gloved hands and peered back through his legs—same as always—to lock in on his target. Punter Ken Walter was ready, his upper torso leaning slightly toward the line of scrimmage, his arms swinging forward and back at his sides, eagerly anticipating the arrival of the ball. When Brian snapped it, he immediately knew that something did not feel right. *Uh-oh.* By compensating to avoid a high ball, Brian had gone too far and thrown a low one. The ball bounced in front of Walter. Thanks to his concentration and good hands—Walter had been a catcher when he played high school baseball—he was able to handle it. But the bad snap clearly forced him out of rhythm and the punt was not pretty, a wobbly twenty-seven yarder that hit the ground with a thud and rolled to a stop at the Tennessee thirty-six-yard line.

Returning to the sideline, Brian knew he was going to be verbally assaulted by his coaches. Sure enough, he was greeted by Belichick and special-teams coach Brad Seely, standing side by side, yelling at him. "Like two hungry wolves, just gouging me—not that I didn't deserve it," Brian would later say.

"What are you *doing?*" Belichick bellowed. "You have one damn job to do!"

Clearly, the honeymoon was over. Up until this point, Brian had felt that Belichick was treating him almost like a long-lost friend rather than a current player. Not anymore. Brian was now reminded of the way Belichick used to get on him in Cleveland when he did something wrong—*as if I had done it on purpose because I didn't like him or something.*

Brian asked a ball boy to catch some practice snaps for him on the sideline, and he concentrated on getting the ball up higher again. Determined to avoid throwing another low one in the game, he worked on the position of his hips and the follow-through of his hands. But nothing would be solved by technique alone. Brian also needed to regain control of his emotions. Stewing on the sideline, he kept replaying the bad snap in his mind, and he felt tremendous pressure not to let it happen again. *Another one on the ground, and my head is on a platter,* Brian figured. Not since his first game snapping as a rookie with the Miami Dolphins, back in 1988, had he ever been so scared during a football game. Brian remained confident about snapping for an extra point or field goal. The shorter snaps did not concern him. But the thought of another punt snap was eating him up, so he made a decision. Next time out, he would take something off the snap and throw the ball to the punter with a slight arc, thereby allowing himself a greater margin of error and decreasing the chance of a costly mistake. Brian could hardly believe that he was resorting to such a cautious tactic. But he had to do it. Stuck in emotional free fall, he felt that he needed to build in some sort of a safety net.

With twenty seconds left in the second quarter, Brian was back on the field for one more test before halftime: another punt snap, from the New England forty-one-yard line. As long as the Patriots' punt team could execute cleanly, the Titans would probably let the final seconds of the half expire without trying to do anything on offense. But if Brian were to make another mistake, the Titans could very well get a shot at a last-second field goal to cut the Patriots' lead to four. *Just do what you do,* Brian told himself.

As planned, he took a little something off the snap. Walter was so focused on doing his own job that he did not even notice. But Patriots offensive coordinator Charlie Weis would later tease Brian that a sundial could have been used to time his delivery. Regardless of what anyone else thought, Brian was satisfied with the snap, and the outcome was perfect. Walter gathered in the ball without incident, punted it away, and Derrick Mason of the Titans made a fair catch at the Tennessee thirty-four-yard line. Mission accomplished. Quarterback Steve McNair took a knee to run out the clock, and Brian was able to exhale as he headed into the locker room with the Patriots still leading by a touchdown.

That did not mean that he would now be free of anxiety for the rest of the night. The next time Brian was called upon to snap, when the Patriots were forced to punt on their first possession of the second half, he threw another bad one, high and to the right of the punter this time. Walter was still able to pick the football out of the air, but he was again forced out of his regular routine, and he managed only twenty-four yards on the punt. Brian felt as if he were dying a thousand deaths as he sought refuge on the sideline and began to wonder why he had ever even thought about returning to the NFL. There was nothing fun about this. He was working in a pressure-packed house of horrors, and now there was only one thing that mattered to him: survival.

Late in the third quarter, McNair hit Mason with an eleven-yard touchdown pass to tie the score at 14–14. The predictions of a close, hard-hitting contest were proving to be correct. This game was going down to the final minutes.

Brian was called on for another punt snap in the fourth quarter, and he threw another "sundial" ball, but right on target this time, and Walter's punt pinned the Titans deep in their own territory. *Made it through another one,* Brian thought. *This has got to be the longest frickin' game of my life.*

The Tennessee offense was unable to gain much ground on the ensuing possession, and New England soon got the ball back at the Tennessee forty-yard line. Seven plays later, with 4:11 left in the game and the score still knotted, Brian and Walter once again made their way onto the field, but this time they had Adam Vinatieri with them. Brian would snap, Walter would hold, and Vinatieri would try to make a forty-six-yard field goal to claim the lead and possibly the game. Quite naturally, all eyes were fixed on Vinatieri, one of the most accomplished clutch kickers in the league. On the CBS broadcast, analyst Phil Simms cited Vinatieri's eight-year career mark—fourteen of nineteen—on game-winning or game-tying field-goal attempts. What Simms did not mention, though, was that Vinatieri was in the midst of his most inconsistent year as a professional. From thirty yards and beyond, he had connected on only nine of eighteen attempts, including his miss earlier in this game. Simms also failed to say anything about the way Brian had been struggling. Why would he? Brian was only a long snapper, invisible, by definition, unless disaster were to strike. How would a television announcer—or anyone else—possibly be aware of the personal hell Brian had been battling since that bounced snap back in the second quarter?

Fortunately for the Patriots, punt snapping was not the issue now. All Brian had to do was deliver the ball from a much shorter distance so that Walter could properly place it for Vinatieri. Brian leaned over the ball on the right hash mark. Walter flashed his right hand to signal that he was ready for the snap. And Brian fired away. The snap was good. The hold was good. And the kick was . . . ball spinning wildly through the air and falling to the left . . . good! Not by much. The ball curled just inside the left upright and barely cleared the crossbar. But the Patriots had the lead, 17–14, and now their defense would be called upon to do the same thing it had been doing so well for months. With the clock running down and the game on the line, it was time to dig in and shut down the opponent.

The Patriots initially yielded significant chunks of yardage, giving up first downs on three consecutive plays, and the two-minute warning came with the Titans threatening at the New England thirty-three-yard line. But the defense stiffened, and two straight penalties pushed the Titans back into their own territory. With 1:45 left, the game came down to a fourth-and-twelve play for Tennessee from the New England forty-two. The Patriots defense, one stop away from ending the Titans' season, would undoubtedly be in attack mode. At the same time, the Titans were only one first down away from being in range for a game-tying field goal. And they would still have plenty of time to go for a touchdown that would probably give them the outright victory. McNair lined up in shotgun formation. Under a heavy rush from his right and about to be hit by blitzing safety Rodney Harrison, he lobbed a pass high in the air to the left, for wide receiver Drew Bennett, who had already made two impressive catches on the drive. Bennett had a clear shot at the ball when he leaped for it at the fifteen-yard line, but his hands inexplicably failed him and the ball bounced harmlessly to the ground. All that remained was for the Patriots to run out the clock on offense.

The battle on the frozen tundra of Foxborough—"a whale of a football game," Belichick called it—belonged to the home team. Patriot fans were thrilled that in eight days they would be returning to Gillette Stadium for the AFC championship game. Coaches and players were equally excited about being only one step away from the Super Bowl. But Brian was hardly in a celebratory mood. More than anything, he was just relieved.

Relieved that he had not done anything horrible to cost his team both the game and the season. Relieved that he had survived what felt to him like the longest game of his life. Relieved that he and the Patriots had lived to fight another day.

Speaking into his tape recorder the next day, Brian said, "My prayer now is for peace of mind, for confidence in what I am doing."

Ten

With the second semester beginning back at Parkview, Brian wanted to tape another installment of what he came to call "video mail" for his students. This time, the Monday after the Tennessee game, a day off for the Patriots players, the purpose was to introduce himself to his new classes. The kids already knew that he was away playing football, and that Lori would still be subbing for him until the Patriots were done for the year (either the following weekend—if they were to lose in the AFC championship game against the Indianapolis Colts—or two weeks after that if they were to win and make it to the Super Bowl). But Brian wanted to have at least some sort of contact with his students as they settled into class without him. After sleeping late and then staying in bed until almost eleven in the morning, he started his day by setting up his camera in the hotel room. The location did not really matter. As was the case when he taped the earlier video in his home office, the shot was so tightly framed on his head that the background was irrelevant. Wearing a white baseball cap with a big, black Nike swoosh across the front of it, Brian looked straight into the camera to "meet" his new students.

"Hello, everyone, my name is Brian Kinchen, your new Bible teacher for this semester," he said. "I want to welcome you all to seventh-grade Bible. I've been looking forward to this semester, as I did last semester. I had a wonderful time with your classmates. And I'm sure we'll have a wonderful time this semester also. I want this to be a time that we can enjoy together . . . getting to know one another."

Brian spoke for a few minutes about the way a regular week of class was going to work. Two days—Tuesday and Thursday— would be dedicated to standard teaching and discussion. Working from a book called *Sticking Up for What I Believe,* Brian would cover a wide range of material that would enable his students to better understand, explain, and defend the underlying tenets of their faith in God. Bible passages and events would also be taught on Tuesday and Thursday. Each of the remaining days would be dedicated to something different. Monday would be chapel day; class would be held in the school sanctuary, and the students would have quiet time to read their Bibles and pray. Wednesday would be focused on the stories of Christian martyrs told in a book called *Jesus Freaks,* co-written by dc Talk, a Grammy Award–winning Christian rock and rap band that was popular with teens. Friday would be ministry day, a time for outreach and special projects, such as making cards for people who were sick or preparing food baskets for elderly people who had difficulty getting out of their apartments or homes.

When he was done laying out the overall structure for his classes, Brian told his students he would take them on a video tour that would offer some insight into what his life was like while he was away from school and his family. "My little world here in New England," he said. "I hope you enjoy it. It's not much. But you'll get to see some things that you normally wouldn't. I'll show you the stadium and the inside of our locker room and things like that . . . things that are maybe somewhat interesting."

One of the first things his new students would learn about Brian was that—at least in the role of documentarian—he was unmistakably a man of minutiae. Before leaving for the stadium, not only did he shoot several camera angles to show the inside of his room at the Residence Inn. While offering a running commentary, he also included the view out his window to the hotel parking lot ("had a little snowfall . . . ground is covered"), an exterior close-up of the door to his suite ("room number one-oh-eight"), and a quick look down his hallway ("I see it every day"). When he got to the lobby, taking a wide shot of the dining area in which he ate breakfast was not sufficient. He also felt obligated to include a tight shot of the waffle iron that had been so good to him.

Taking the students with him on his way to Gillette Stadium— his left hand on the steering wheel, right hand holding and aiming the camera—Brian casually delivered play-by-play of his daily drive. "Here we are with a view out of my van window as I go to work," he said. "First flashing red light of the day, where I make a left." Then, after a brief break in the commentary, he identified another less-than-dramatic landmark: "The underpass that I go through every day." Brian continued the cinematic adventure with equally gripping footage of a traffic circle, a few more turns, and a Dairy Queen that always let him know he was headed in the right direction. Clearly aware that his tour was not exactly climaxing just yet, Brian self-mockingly intoned, "This is real-life stuff here, people."

Luckily for the students, Brian soon offered them an upgrade in the form of Gillette Stadium, which first became visible through a wooded area along a residential street shortly before he would turn onto U.S. Route 1. "The *Razor*," Brian said, invoking a popular nickname for the mammoth two-year-old stadium that also served as the core of the Patriots' training complex. "Beautiful facility." Once there, the tour picked up with an up-close look at the inner sanctums of a professional football team: The dining area in which Brian had been sitting four weeks earlier when Belichick first told him he was going to be a New England Patriot. The team meeting room into which Brian had walked so sheepishly during his first day on the job. The locker room—including a shot of a big Patriots logo designed into the carpet and a look into the neatly kept stall that housed his belongings. The equipment room. The weight room. The training room. Once again employing his keen eye for the truly mundane, Brian even captured shots of the sinks and showers used by the Patriots. "Ton of room in here, for a ton of guys," he said while slowly panning the empty shower room. When Brian was done showing his students around the inside facilities, he took them out to the playing field. The stands were empty, save for a few workers starting to get things ready for the big game against the Colts. Brian captured footage of the Patriots' sideline and noted where their benches would be lined up for a game. He showed a few television people setting up for a field-level interview in a corner of the stadium. He zoomed in on a grounds crew rolling up a giant tarp that had been covering the field. And then—stadium tour concluded—Brian went back inside.

Without the camera rolling, he wanted to take care of a little business. Brian sought out Brad Seely so he could talk to the special-teams coach about his punt snapping in the Tennessee game. Actually, what Brian really wanted to do was say he was sorry for how poorly he had performed against the Titans. Seely was low-key and understanding, but the only thing that really mattered to him was figuring out how to correct the problem. All the apologies in the world would never do a thing for the Patriots. The only thing Seely ever wanted from a long snapper—ever *needed*—could easily be summed up in one word: *accuracy*.

On his way out of Gillette Stadium, Brian went back to taping for his students. His tour continued with a trip to his favorite neighborhood movie house, Showcase Cinemas, to see *Big Fish* on the big screen. "I'll let you know how it goes," Brian promised. It was dark outside by the time he was back to his van and his video camera. "Good movie," he said. And then he immediately returned to his memorialization of the inane, showing his students an Italian restaurant (Bertucci's) where he liked to eat, a small grocery store (Tedeschi Food Shops) where he sometimes picked up ice cream and other snacks, and a video store (Blockbuster) where he rented movies. "I picked up *Antwone Fisher* to watch tonight," Brian said. "That's the highlight of my evening."

Brian would later edit his video mail to close with additional remarks—back to the tight shot in the Nike hat—taped in his hotel room: "Well, I told you it wasn't going to be much. But it was something at least to let you get an insight of what I'm doing, and where I'm living, and how I'm getting along here without my family, whom I miss *so* very much. And I miss being there with you guys. Now . . . be sure and behave for Miss Lori until I get back home. And I'll see you—hopefully after the Super Bowl. Thanks."

Brian could not explain the way he was feeling. Part of it had to be the football-related pressure that was building, with the bad game against Tennessee still haunting him and the AFC championship game against the Colts only days away—a combination that created both great excitement and tremendous vulnerability. Part of it had to be the result of being away from his wife and children for so long, off on his own, other than brief visits, for a full month now; "kind of lonely," he confided to his audio journal. And perhaps some of it could even be attributed to the movies he was watching, *Big Fish* being an emotional father-son story that pushed him deep into thought about his own relationships and life, and *Antwone Fisher* being a tear-jerker about a troubled young man who had been abandoned and abused as a child. Whatever the reason, one thing was clear about the week leading up to the AFC championship game: for Brian, it was a time of heavy introspection.

He was drawn back into a book—*The Man in the Mirror*—that he had been reading in Baton Rouge as part of a men's discussion group at his church. Written by Patrick M. Morley and first published in 1989, it is a popular Christian book aimed at addressing "the problems, issues, and temptations" that come with being a man. Brian and his group had already worked through the first four chapters. Now he took a solo journey into the fifth, a thirteen-page look at a question—"Purpose: Why Do I Exist?"—that could easily cover the whole shelf of a library without ever reaching a definitive answer. Morley had concluded that it is essential for one to understand the difference between goals and purpose.

"One of the gripping problems men face is that achieving goals becomes an unrelated string of hollow victories, increasingly frustrating as more and more is achieved," he wrote. "That's the problem with goals: you have to keep setting new ones because achieving them doesn't provide any lasting satisfaction."

Brian did not like to mark the pages of a book. Why mess up a perfectly good volume? But he was nonetheless locked in on that passage, fully aware that he needed to do more than just read it once and then forget about it. The words spoke directly to him. All his life, he had been a goal setter. All his life, he had been focused on specific achievements and had always measured his self-worth based on some sort of murky, performance-related scale. By living that way, he could never do quite well enough, could never be quite good enough. Brian always knew there had to be a better way. As genuinely spiritual as he was, though, he had never been able to figure out how to find it and fully embrace it, how to truly *live* it.

"To be satisfying," Morley continued, "our goals need to reflect our examination of life's larger meaning. The plain truth is that most men don't know their purpose in life, or their purpose is too small. A man can do nothing more important than to wrestle with the purpose of his life."

There was so much more that really got Brian thinking.

"Purposes are *threads of continuity* that we weave into the long-term view of our lives."

"Purposes are a place to begin. They help us focus our lives and give them direction so our goals do not become an unrelated string of hollow victories."

"Goals are what we do. Purposes are why we do what we do."

At the end of the chapter, Brian found a worksheet for developing a life-purpose statement of his own. He read what Morley had to say on the subject. He thought about it for a while. Then he reached for another book he had with him—this one he was never without for very long—and he also grabbed a pencil from the desk in his hotel room. Brian was ready to break his personal rule about writing in a book. He flipped to a blank page in the back of his Bible, the same Thompson Chain-Reference Bible he had used ever since his maternal grandparents ("Grammie" and "Gramps") had given it to him during the summer of 1985, and put pencil to paper. Under the heading "Life Purpose Statement" and the date "1–14–04" (the Wednesday before the biggest football game of his life), Brian wrote: "To continually seek God's heart, and share Him with the world through the love and respect I give to everyone around me. Loving and raising my children to have hearts for God and to be my living legacy in this world and the next."

A short while later, Brian was saying good night to his children by telephone, telling them how much he loved them, and his third son, Logan, hit him out of nowhere with an innocent question that felt like a kick to the gut.

"Dad, are you going to be home for my birthday?"

Logan would be turning eight in five days, on Monday the nineteenth, the day after the game against the Colts.

"I hate to say it, but if we win, I don't think I'll be able to make it," Brian said.

"You won't?" Logan said.

"Does that make you sad?"

"Yes."

"I'm sorry, Logan. But don't worry, I'll still be sending a present for you, and I'll see you soon. I promise, okay?"

"Okay."

But was it really? Brian had long felt that being a dad, always being there for his boys when they wanted or needed him, was his greatest purpose in this world. Now he was feeling the hurt of missing Logan's birthday while sitting alone in a faraway hotel room . . . sitting there because he had temporarily made football a priority over everything else. In all the excitement of returning to the NFL, Brian had never considered what it would be like to be gone for Logan's birthday. It had never even dawned on him that he would be away for such an important occasion—and there was nothing he could do about it now. Soon after hanging up the phone, Brian felt the moisture starting to pool in his eyes.

In all his previous years of professional football—thirteen seasons with the Miami Dolphins, Cleveland Browns, Baltimore Ravens, and Carolina Panthers—Brian had never felt the need to give himself a daily report card on how he was snapping in practice. Why would he have? To borrow the analogy that Brian often used, snapping had for him always been like riding a bicycle, and, Lance Armstrong types aside, who in the world would ever need to evaluate and chronicle how well he was doing on a bicycle? There was no need to think about it a whole lot. Just hop on and go.

But everything was different now. Brian had never before experienced a game like the one he had against Tennessee. He had never before faced the pressure of a game as big as the AFC championship. All the routines and rituals of a game week, normally just taken for granted, were now under a microscope, every action and reaction being carefully dissected and analyzed. And so Brian could not help himself. After each of the final few practices leading up to the game against the Colts, he shared with his audio journal a self-critique of his day's work. His snapping on Wednesday was "really good." It was a huge relief to feel like he was back to normal again. Thursday was "another good day." And Friday was "pretty decent."

The only notable aberration was a low ball Brian threw while the team was working on field goals—and Belichick immediately getting on him about needing to get the ball up. "I know that!" Brian angrily yelled back. That prompted some raised eyebrows on the practice field. It also brought a few chuckles from some of the players. It was not often that someone spoke back to Belichick. "In retrospect, it was not very respectful, I guess," Brian conceded when speaking into his tape recorder that night. "But I was more yelling at myself than anything."

That aside, though, Brian sure felt a whole lot better after a predominantly good week of practice than he had coming out of that first playoff game against Tennessee. Lori, Austin, and Hunter were back in town again for the weekend, and Brian was determined to temporarily put the upcoming game out of his mind so that he could enjoy being with them. Saturday afternoon, Brian and the boys took a long walk in the woods behind the hotel, very much enjoying the snow and ice of New England, a special treat for father and sons from the Deep South. That evening, shortly before Ken Walter was to pick up Brian to take him to the hotel where the Patriots stayed the night before a game, Lori gave her husband a big hug and looked straight into his eyes.

"Are you nervous?" she asked.

"Well, of course," Brian said. "I mean, same as always. But there is also the added pressure because I went so long without doing this, so much time away from football, and then there is also the whole thought that there is so much riding on the game."

"You'll do great," Lori said. She was not really worried about his ability to snap under pressure. She was more concerned about the possibility of the Patriots having an off day and his football dreams dying once again—one final time—without a trip to the Super Bowl. But she also knew Brian well enough to know that he was worrying way too much about his own performance. "You've snapped perfectly for thirteen years," Lori said. "Just do it the way you always have."

"I had a good week," Brian said. "I feel good about it." After a slight pause, still gazing at the only woman with whom he had ever truly been in love, he ended the conversation with this: "I have confidence in my ability. And I have confidence that God will provide me with whatever I need to get my job done."

Eleven

The Patriots already knew everything they needed to know about the high-powered Colts. All anyone in New England had to do was think back to the titanic regular-season clash between the longtime rivals—with Indianapolis quarterback Peyton Manning throwing three straight second-half touchdown passes and looking like he was about to pull off one of the most remarkable comeback victories of the season, only to be defeated when the Patriots dug in and made that gutty goal-line stand in the final seconds. The Colts had lost only one more game after that, finishing the regular season with a record of 12–4, and that was nothing compared with what they had just done in their first two playoff games. In defeating the Denver Broncos at home and the Kansas City Chiefs on the road, Manning & Company, also featuring fellow Pro Bowlers Edgerrin James at running back and Marvin Harrison at wide receiver, had exploded for a combined total of seventy-nine points. Manning had passed for 681 yards and eight touchdowns without any interceptions. Perhaps the most impressive statistic reflected something that the Colts had *not* done. In two games, they had not once been forced to punt the ball away. Clearly, they had the most potent offense of anybody left in the playoffs.

On the other hand, although Manning had recently been named co-MVP of the NFL (along with Steve McNair of the Titans), he was now six years into his professional career without a victory over New England in Foxborough. He had lost four times there, with a dismal overall record of 2–7 against the Patriots. In addition, the Patriots were now playing the best defense they had ever played—the most stifling defense in the entire NFL. No team had allowed as few points, 14.9 per game, during the regular season. And the Patriots had been especially tough at home, giving up only 8.5 points per game, without ever losing in Gillette Stadium. It was with good reason that some of the Patriots had started to wear blue caps with white letters proclaiming: "Homeland Defense."

With the AFC championship game set for three o'clock the afternoon of Sunday, January 18—and with a spot in Super Bowl XXXVIII weighing in the balance—one did not need a whole lot of football knowledge to understand that something would have to give on one side of the ball. As *Boston Globe* columnist Bob Ryan put it: "Has there ever been an easier game to frame? Colts offense vs. Patriots defense."

This time it was snow instead of arctic chill that greeted the Patriots on game day. But it was nothing they had not seen before, and after facing such extreme conditions a week earlier against the Titans, just about anything would be an upgrade. The Colts, who played their home games indoors, were not overjoyed by the winter weather in New England, but the temperature of thirty-one degrees felt downright balmy for the Patriots. Pre-game warm-up went very well for Brian. He snapped without any problem and felt entirely comfortable. What a day this was going to be! He had tremendous faith in his teammates. He had never before felt so good about a team he was on. And the Patriots were only one victory away from the proverbial promised land—sixty minutes of playing time away from the Super Bowl.

The Patriots got the ball first and went right through the Colts on a thirteen-play drive that culminated in a seven-yard touchdown pass from Tom Brady to David Givens. The snap and the kick were good, and the Patriots had an early 7–0 lead. Now came the hard part: stopping the Colts. On their first offensive play of the game, Peyton Manning connected with tight end Marcus Pollard for a thirty-two-yard completion to the New England forty-six-yard line. "Game on!" the Colts seemed to be saying. Eight plays later, they were threatening at the five. But Manning, again targeting Pollard, was intercepted by safety Rodney Harrison in the end zone.

The Patriots went on another impressive drive, but they eventually stalled at the Indianapolis thirteen-yard line and had to settle for a field-goal attempt. Perfect snap. Perfect kick. All systems were go for both Brian (two routine snaps to start his day) and the Patriots (10–0 lead early in the second quarter).

Manning and the Colts were determined to return to the type of productivity that had come so easily for them in the early rounds of the playoffs. On the very next play from scrimmage, however, cornerback Ty Law made an acrobatic, leaping catch of a pass intended for Marvin Harrison, and the Patriots had the ball right back. After two entire playoff games without throwing a single interception, Manning had now been picked off on two consecutive passes. The turnover led to another field goal by the Patriots and a margin of 13–0.

The Patriots defense continued to play very physically—constantly looking to rough up the much-heralded Indianapolis receivers, who had for weeks been running their patterns so freely—and the Colts appeared to be totally out of sync. With 4:13 left in the first half, they were forced to do something they had not done since the regular season. Facing fourth-and-ten at their own thirty-five-yard line, the Colts finally called on their punt team. Hunter Smith ("Hunter the Punter," as he was often called) stood with his feet slightly staggered, right heel on the twenty-yard line, and readied himself for action. With fourth-year long snapper Justin Snow leaning over the ball, there was no need for Smith to think about the way it would be delivered to him. That very week he had told a *New York Times* writer, "Justin's the best punt-snapper in the league. I've never had a bad punt snap from him." Much to the dismay of Hunter the Punter, however, the snap from Snow now sailed high above his head. Smith jumped for the ball, but he could only barely get his extended fingers on it. Then he was off to the races, turning and chasing after the bouncing ball in the hopes of reaching it before the Patriots could (either picking it up and running it in for a touchdown or—at the least—pouncing on it and giving their offense the ball with an immediate first-and-goal opportunity to score another seven points). Smith caught up with the ball at the eight-yard line, where it was still rolling a bit, and he kicked it straight through the end zone for a safety. It was yet another ugly blow for the Colts, giving up two more points and now trailing 15–0. It was a wide-awake nightmare for Snow, instantly creating a career lowlight while playing in the biggest game of his life.

Speaking over slow-motion replay of the bad snap and the safety, CBS analyst Phil Simms said, "Well, the wet football, we've seen a couple instances where it's gotten away from the quarterbacks, and this time it gets away from the Colts' long snapper. Good job by Hunter Smith. Just give up the two points and get the football out of play." Simms had temporarily allowed Snow to remain unidentified to the national television audience, but his broadcast partner, Greg Gumbel, soon took care of that. "Justin Snow was the *long* snapper," Gumbel said. "And he did just that."

Standing on the sideline, Brian felt no burst of joy from the two points the Patriots had just been gifted. What he experienced was more of a sinking feeling for someone he had never even met, an empathetic emptiness. By job description alone, Brian and Snow were brethren, each one every bit a competitor seeking only what was best for his team, of course, but they also shared an alliance of unspoken familiarity—a blind bond that automatically made them colleagues. *Can't even imagine how horrible he must feel,* Brian thought. As much as he had himself struggled in the Tennessee game, at least he had not done anything that ended up hurting his team. And the stakes were so much higher now. One step away from the Super Bowl! If the Colts were to fight their way back into the game—and if those two points from the safety were to end up directly affecting the outcome—Snow would not exactly be the toast of the town in Indianapolis.

The Colts began the second half by finally putting points on the scoreboard with a twelve-play touchdown drive, capping it off with a two-yard run by Edgerrin James. But the Patriots' offense came up with two more field goals in the third quarter, and their defense kept hounding Manning and his receivers into costly mistakes. After that opening score in the second half, the Colts' next three possessions ended in nothing but futility: Three plays that went nowhere and then a punt on the first. Two more interceptions by Ty Law on the second and third. Not only was Law taking away the football; he appeared to be stealing the whole show.

Still, though the Patriots had both the ball and a 21–7 lead more than midway through the fourth quarter, nobody was about to count out the high-octane offense of the Colts. With 6:16 left in the game, the Patriots finally had to punt for the first time. Brian's snap was not perfect—a little off to the right—but Ken Walter handled it with no problem and booted the ball away. After a fair catch at their own thirty-three-yard line, the Colts were clearly in a do-or-die situation. Running a no-huddle offense, Manning marched his team down the field and into the end zone—on a seven-yard touchdown pass to Marcus Pollard—to make it 21–14. With 2:27 remaining, the Colts still had enough time for late-game heroics, and they tried to get the ball right back with an onside kick. It did not work. But the Patriots went nowhere on three straight plays and had to punt. Starting at their own twenty-yard line, the Colts had 2:01 to score a touchdown and push the game into overtime. Twenty times in his six-year career, nine of them in the previous two seasons alone, Manning had led his team on game-winning drives in the fourth quarter or overtime. But now he faced one of the best defenses in NFL history, and the Patriots went into full lockdown mode. After four straight incomplete passes, the ball once again belonged to New England. With fifty-five seconds to play, the Patriots kicked yet another field goal, increasing their margin to 24–14, and then the game belonged to them as well.

Fourteen wins in a row! One more game to go!

For the second time in three years, the New England Patriots were on their way to the Super Bowl. Tom Brady unleashed a big smile and triumphantly raised his arms high into the air. Bill Belichick turned toward the jubilant crowd and lifted his left fist for the adoring fans. Fireworks lit up the otherwise dark sky high above the stadium.

Brian could hardly believe the whole thing. He was excited about celebrating with his teammates; he genuinely felt like part of the team by this point. But first there was something else he wanted to do. He wanted to console the only other guy on the field who did the same job that he did. Brian had been thinking about Justin Snow ever since Snow had thrown that high snap that cost the Colts so dearly in the second quarter. Brian felt awful for him, felt awful *with* him. *Could very well be me.* And so he sought out Snow as the Colts were heading to the visitors' locker room. After shaking hands, the two long snappers walked together, slowly, for about ten yards. Brian had no idea if Snow had ever even known of him, no idea if the twenty-seven-year-old "youngster" had any clue that he was a veteran of fourteen NFL seasons and was speaking from what felt like a lifetime's worth of experience. And none of that really mattered now; all Brian cared about was reaching out with some sort of affirmation.

"You've been doing a great job," he told Snow. "Don't beat yourself up over one play."

"Thanks," Snow said. "I really appreciate it."

By the time Brian turned back to his teammates, some of them were already wearing AFC championship hats. A portable stage was being set up on the field for the presentation of the Lamar Hunt Trophy that went to the conference champion. Brian was ready to whoop it up a bit. And why not? To call this a dream come true would have been underselling the magnitude of the moment. What man in his right mind ever would have dreamed of something like this—such an improbable path to the Super Bowl? Brian had already considered himself amazingly fortunate just to get an unexpected second chance at professional football, simply to be able to play again and then retire on his own terms. Now this. Other than winning the lottery, he could not imagine a quicker or more euphoric ascent. *Surreal*—that was the only way Brian would ever be able to describe what he was seeing and thinking and feeling as the celebration continued.

Standing only a few yards from the stage, Brian had his own personal moment of reflection when he looked up and realized who had been chosen to make the trophy presentation to Patriots owner Robert Kraft. It was Larry Csonka, the old Miami Dolphins running back from the 1970s, the player Brian had admired most on his favorite childhood team. With the upcoming Super Bowl to be played in Houston, the NFL had selected Csonka to participate as a way to commemorate the thirty-year anniversary of the last time the game had been played there, when Csonka had been named MVP of Super Bowl VIII. No matter which way Brian turned on his unimaginable, magical journey with the Patriots, the serendipitous gifts just kept on coming.

After the trophy presentation, Jim Nantz of CBS conducted brief interviews with some of the central figures for the Patriots:

Bill Belichick, Tom Brady, Ty Law, Antowain Smith, Rodney Harrison. When Nantz was done, though, it was one of the final shots before going to commercial that would have really lit up the diligent and knowing eyes of any seventh grader who attended Parkview back in Baton Rouge. Because right there on national television was a celebratory shot of a player almost nobody else ever would have recognized or known. To the average football fan, he was just some generic ballplayer wrapped in jersey number forty-six. To the Parkview kids, he was so much more than that. He was Mr. Kinchen or Mr. Brian. He was Coach or Professor. He was *their* guy in the NFL, their personal link to the entirely foreign and grand world of celebrity. The closing glimpse of Brian came as he was hugging and speaking with teammate Jarvis Green, a fellow LSU alum, who had just completed the game of his life. A second-year player primarily used throughout the season in a backup role at defensive end, Green had been inserted into the middle of a special defensive alignment the Patriots had designed to use against the Colts, and he had responded by sacking Peyton Manning three times—the first time anyone in the NFL had ever done that to Manning in a single game. Both Brian and Green were wearing big smiles now. They had no idea they were on television screens all over the country. But they would soon be playing on the biggest stage in all of American sports.

Twelve

Logan Kinchen began his eighth birthday with a sweet and doughy breakfast of beignets, a deep-fried Louisiana specialty that would make just about any kid happy. With his mom and dad out of town—this was Monday, January 19, the morning after the Patriots–Colts game—his paternal grandparents, Toni and Gus Kinchen, were watching after him. And with "Meme" and "Poppe" running the show, Logan was living large at one of the most popular coffee shops in the area, Coffee Call, where he got all the powdered sugar he could possibly want on those beignets. Not a bad way to celebrate his birthday. Logan was also allowed to miss school and goof around all day. But none of that would get him what he really wanted, which was to see his dad, and Logan had no idea that Brian would soon be doing everything he could to make that happen.

Lori was on her way back from Boston with Austin and Hunter. Brian was at Gillette Stadium, where he had already gone through an early-morning workout in the weight room and was now in a team meeting. Bill Belichick was discussing logistics for the next two weeks, leading up to the Super Bowl. He offered information about travel and hotel rooms and game tickets. For Brian, the best thing that came out of the meeting was learning that once Belichick was done speaking, the players would be off until Thursday morning. Then they would practice for three days before flying to Houston on Sunday, January 25, one week before playing the Carolina Panthers in Super Bowl XXXVIII.

Brian immediately began plotting a trip to Louisiana. He was eager to sleep in his own bed. He looked forward to seeing everyone at school. What he wanted most of all was to share at least a piece of Logan's birthday with him. Brian was able to get a flight out in the late afternoon. Much to his disappointment, however, he did not make it home until well after Logan's bedtime.

After exchanging a quick hello with Lori—they had just been together that morning in Massachusetts—Brian hurried upstairs to the safari-themed bedroom that Logan shared with four-year-old McKane. It contained enough stuffed animals and jungle-related knickknacks to stock the gift shop of a zoo. With a colorful variety of lions, tigers, and elephants staring at him from framed prints on the walls, Brian quietly approached the right side of the queen-size bed that swallowed up his two youngest boys. Logan was out cold. So was McKane. But just seeing those little guys, so peaceful and content in the dark of night, cherubic chests expanding and contracting ever so slightly with each obliviously drawn breath of air—that alone was enough to hold Brian still for a minute and make him feel whole.

Brian did not want to disturb Logan's sleep just because a bit of his birthday still remained on the clock. He could certainly wait until the morning to visit with his son. But he was not yet ready to leave the room. Brian leaned over the bed and gently kissed his birthday boy on the cheek. "Love you, buddy," he whispered. Then he placed one hand on Logan's chest and the other on McKane's, and he softly prayed out loud: "Thank you, Lord, for allowing me to be here with Logan on his birthday. Thank you for all my boys. Please watch over them as they sleep. Please give them sweet dreams, and no bad dreams. I pray that they rest well, have a wonderful day tomorrow, and honor you with all that they do."

Brian tucked in the bed coverings. He navigated his way past all those wild animals that never made a move without the help of a Kinchen. And he went downstairs to be with Lori.

If Brian ever wanted to illustrate for someone who knew nothing about his sport the vast differences between the regular-guy life of a low-man-on-the-totem-pole long snapper and the high-profile existence of a big-time NFL quarterback, he would only have to describe the events of his first complete day back in Baton Rouge, Tuesday, January 20. After visiting with his boys first thing in the morning, virtually shadowing them until they left for school, Brian went by himself to a nearby gym and lifted weights. Then he showered and headed over to Parkview, where he spent a few hours casually visiting with students and staff. Everyone seemed genuinely happy to see him. Both the kids and the adults also expressed great joy *for* him, pretty much every man, woman, and child in the school community now fully aware that one of their own would soon be playing in the Super Bowl. But there was no brass band or organized ceremony to announce his presence—and there certainly was no public recognition from the leader of the free world.

That evening, Brian relaxed at home and watched George W. Bush deliver the annual State of the Union address to the U.S. Congress and a national television audience. The president spoke about the war on terror and specifically about the U.S. commitment in Iraq. He offered his thoughts on major domestic issues such as the economy, education, and health care. And then he touched on a much narrower topic: the use of performance-enhancing steroids in baseball, football, and other sports. Brian was surprised to hear the president use such a major forum to "call on team owners, union representatives, coaches, and players to take the lead, to send the right signal, to get tough, and to get rid of steroids now." What came as an even bigger surprise was seeing a live shot of teammate Tom Brady, wrapped in a dark suit and tie, enjoying a bird's-eye view from the balcony box of First Lady Laura Bush while her husband was speaking about steroids and the need for "good examples" in athletics. "You get invited, you go," Brady would later tell reporters. "It was a great honor. It was way cool."

And so there it was—an extremely telling juxtaposition of activities on the same day off for two members of the same football team: the long snapper visiting with kids at a middle school in Baton Rouge, Louisiana, then settling down on a couch and watching television; the star quarterback mingling with the power elite at the White House, then heading over to the U.S. Capitol and serving as a prop for the president during one of the biggest political events of the year. Who would ever need any further explanation to understand the tremendously different lives of one man who throws footballs between his legs without anyone knowing his name and another who throws them while upright and with all sorts of cameras focused on his every move?

The next morning, Brian and Lori went with their students to the regular weekly chapel session attended by the entire middle school, sixth through eighth grades, which included more than three hundred kids and their teachers. Eighth-grade teacher Sonya Pruitt, who directed the middle school Bible program, stood in the front of the sanctuary and did the best she could to touch young hearts with her messages of hope and faith. She was the same woman who had been such a hit in the school video Lori had made for Brian, the one who had held up that newspaper story and teased Brian about his use of the word *chilling*. Pruitt did not have anything special planned for the Kinchens this time. As chapel was winding down, though, something hit her and she decided to close by inviting them to the front of the room. She also asked Austin (who was there with his fellow eighth graders) and Hunter (then a sixth grader) to join them, and she soon had a quartet of Kinchens at her side.

Standing with them in front of the pulpit, a few steps down from it and now on the same level as everyone else, Pruitt spoke to the room: "What a special time for the Kinchen family. This will be the last chance we get to see Mr. Kinchen before he goes back to his team and then goes to play in the Super Bowl. What a great opportunity to show our love and support, to pray for the whole family. If you would like to come gather around and show your support, then let's do that. You can come on down, and we'll pray together."

The Kinchens were soon engulfed by a throng of students and teachers. Pruitt placed one of her hands on Brian's shoulder and the other on Lori's hands, which she held together. Anyone who was close enough laid hands on a Kinchen or two. Everyone else just placed a hand or hands on anyone within reach. And all bowed their heads. "Heavenly Father, thank you so much for sharing the Kinchen family with us," Pruitt began. She thanked God for giving Brian such a wonderful platform—all the attention of the Super Bowl—to share with the world his deep faith and his heart for God. She asked that Brian be able to use such a great opportunity for whatever purposes God might have in mind. And she prayed for God's protection over the entire Kinchen family as they continued together on their fabulous football journey. "We know that this is not about winning or losing a game," Pruitt said. "It is about being the person who you want us to be. It is about glorifying you. Your word tells us that you will never leave us or forsake us. So we know that as Brian heads off to this game, you will be right there with him, and we thank you for that."

Brian and Lori had tears in their eyes.

Later in the day, a television crew from WAFB, the CBS affiliate in Baton Rouge, visited Parkview to prepare what it called a "Hometown Hero" segment on Brian for the evening news. The reporter wanted to talk about football. Brian was more interested in talking about how much it meant to him to see his students, to hug them, to hear how much they missed him and cared about him. With camera rolling, he said, "There's nothing that can ever hold a candle to that."

The phone calls from friends and acquaintances kept coming. That meant a lot to Brian, and he especially enjoyed hearing from certain people with whom he'd been out of contact for years: old childhood friends, college buddies, guys with whom he had played on other NFL teams. One of the calls that affected him the most came from former NFL kicker Al Del Greco, with whom Brian had developed a friendship while both were playing golf tournaments as members of the Celebrity Players Tour. It was nothing unusual to hear from Del Greco. They spoke fairly often. But now that Brian was headed to the Super Bowl, his golfing buddy had some advice for him.

"Whatever you do, whatever happens during the whole week and during the game itself, just make sure you soak it all in and enjoy every second of it," Del Greco said. "After all those years, you're finally there. What an unbelievable opportunity, what an experience for you and Lori, and for the kids. I don't care how hectic or crazy it gets. The biggest thing you have to promise yourself, win, lose, whatever happens, is that you're going to take it all in and enjoy every single aspect of it—every feeling, every moment, everything you see and do."

Del Greco was speaking with the benefit of experience. On January 30, 2000, after a remarkably long run of sixteen seasons in the NFL, he finally got to play in his first Super Bowl, with the Tennessee Titans. Before going to Atlanta for the week leading up to the game, Del Greco made a pact with himself that he was going to do exactly what he was now suggesting to Brian. "No matter what happens, I'm not going to get all freaked out," he told himself. "I just want to enjoy the ride and see where it goes." Del Greco did not want his Super Bowl experience to be defined only by the outcome of the game against the St. Louis Rams. He also wanted to be sure that he and his family—his wife, Lisa, and their three children, then ages twelve, ten, and six—would be able to bottle up and store away the memories of everything they would be doing that week. Del Greco even decided to carry around a video camera and capture all the images he could. When the game was finally played, he felt both terrible frustration (one missed field goal and another blocked in the first half) and absolute joy (a forty-three-yard field goal that capped a dramatic sixteen-point comeback and temporarily tied the score, 16–16, with only 2:12 left in the game). The Titans ultimately lost on a stunning, seventy-three-yard touchdown pass from Kurt Warner to Isaac Bruce. Although horribly disappointed, Del Greco was at least able to go home with a bundle of wonderful memories that would always be with him.

Four years later, retired from football and living with his family in Birmingham, Alabama, Del Greco knew he would never have any regrets about the way he had approached Super Bowl XXXIV. Sure, he would have loved to walk away with a victory and a ring. But he was thankful that he had intentionally and strategically savored every moment of the experience.

"That's the whole idea," Del Greco told Brian. "You're right where you've always wanted to be. So enjoy it. Just soak it all up and enjoy it."

Brian appreciated the advice. He knew that he still had work to do and would need to stay focused on the job at hand. But now he also had an overall plan for how to approach the biggest week of his football career.

Thirteen

Brian could not have been in a better frame of mind as he headed back to New England for the final days of practice leading up to Super Bowl week. Telling himself that any glitches with his snapping were behind him—and truly believing it—he was intent on following the Del Greco plan. *You're finally here . . . right where you always wanted to be. Enjoy!*

His enjoyment did not last long. On his first morning back at Gillette Stadium, Thursday, January 22, ten days before the Super Bowl, Brian was caught off guard by the way special-teams coach Brad Seely greeted him. "I'm on a rampage today," Seely said. "We can't have snaps to this side, that side, high, low. We have to get them right."

Brian reminded himself of something he had long before concluded about football coaches: the bigger the game, the tighter they get, and they're usually not real good about keeping that to themselves. Brian knew that there was only one way to answer Seely's challenge—going out to practice and throwing perfect snaps.

He failed to do so. On the third field-goal attempt of the day, Brian threw the ball over the head of holder Ken Walter. Out came the attack dogs. Belichick, spitting out his words, was the first one Brian heard: "It all starts with you, Brian!" Then came Seely: "Exactly what we talked about! Time to get it right!" Brian felt awful. The best he could remember, it was only the second time he had ever thrown one completely over the head of a holder. It had happened during the tryout on December 16, and now this one—a grand total of twice in fourteen years. Why now? Was it just a fluke? Nerves? Or was it the unthinkable—that he was somehow losing a gift that had always been his?

Brian got through the rest of practice without anything bad happening. But he was nonetheless rattled. After practice, while everyone else showered and dressed, Brian got a ball from the equipment room and went off by himself to a secluded area in a corridor beneath the stands of the stadium. He was so ashamed of himself, so disgusted with himself. He did not want anyone to see or even know what he was doing. He stepped off eight yards, the distance he and Walter used for a field-goal snap, and spent about fifteen minutes throwing into a wall. "Just to kind of pay penance . . . and make sure I got it right," Brian would later say into his tape recorder.

After throwing thirty snaps, Brian went into the weight room, where he ran into Seely. Brian apologized for the snap over Walter's head and assured his position coach that he was certainly trying his best.

"I know that," Seely said. "I know you're not *trying* to screw up. But it really hurts us if you do that in the game. We just can't have it."

"Yeah, well, neither one of us wants it to happen," Brian said. "The only difference is that I'm the one who has to live with it."

"So do I," Seely said. "Believe me, so do I."

The next day in practice, Brian sailed another field-goal snap over Walter's head. This time, whatever his coaches said in response, whatever they yelled, did not even register with him. He was too far gone in his own little world, shocked, absolutely stunned. He could analyze the situation as much as he wanted, talking to himself about the position of his shoulders, his back, his butt, and trying to solve the problem by focusing on angles and mechanics. But Brian also had to wonder about an entirely different part of the body—his head. How much of this was physical and how much of it was mental? Was he simply stressing too much, hurting himself by thinking and worrying too much about something that had always come so naturally to him? Brian kept trying to convince himself that he was okay, that everything would be fine in time for the Super Bowl. But he also feared the worst: that his confidence was shattered and his whole psyche was falling apart. Unless he could somehow make things right again in the next week, he could very well be heading into a dramatically different Super Bowl experience than the one he had always envisioned for himself. Instead of ending his career on the highest of highs, he could just as easily be approaching a valley of irrevocable nightmares and anguish.

Brian felt like he was about to burst with anxiety. He needed to talk to someone with whom he could be entirely open, someone he could trust to listen and understand without judging. Once he was done at the stadium, he went to a late lunch with Mark Bavaro, his old friend from the Cleveland Browns. Bavaro, the former All-Pro tight end, had been out of the NFL for nine years. But he lived in the Boston area, had always stayed in touch with Belichick, and had been hanging around with the Patriots quite a bit, usually coming by the stadium once or twice a week to watch practice and visit with friends. When Brian joined the Patriots, he and Bavaro were surprised and pleased to see each other again, and whenever Bavaro stopped by practice, they spent some time together. At the age of thirty-eight, Brian had a whole lot more in common with the forty-year-old Bavaro than he did with most of the guys on the team. And they could both laugh about the way things had changed since the 1992 season they had shared in Cleveland. Back then, Bavaro was getting most of the playing time at tight end and Brian, in the role of seldom-used backup, often felt twinges of envy. Now Brian was living what Bavaro considered to be a fairy-tale story with the Patriots, back in the NFL after being out for so long, and going to the Super Bowl, of all things—and Bavaro was the one who felt a touch of jealousy. He was working for an equity trading firm and had long since given up any idea of playing football again. But he had never stopped missing it. That was why he appreciated that Belichick had been so welcoming, letting him come by whenever he wanted and allowing him to feel like he was still connected to the sport he loved.

At lunch, sitting across from Bavaro in a booth at a casual sea-food restaurant not far from the stadium, Brian did more talking than eating. Whatever envy Bavaro had felt quickly disappeared. He had already known that Brian had been struggling a bit—more than one of the coaches had mentioned to him that Brian's snaps had been getting weak and erratic—but he had no idea the extent to which his friend's confidence had been undermined. The way

Brian spoke about the pressure of having to snap in the Super Bowl, with so much at stake and absolutely dreading the possibility of screwing up everything for his team, had Bavaro actually wondering if his friend might be on the verge of a nervous breakdown.

"I don't even want to go," Brian said. "I don't think I can do it."

"Brian, it's too late, man, you got to do it," Bavaro said. "Just relax. You've been doing this forever. You just have to relax and get yourself together."

"Yeah, I know you're right," Brian said. "But I'm still trying to figure out how to do that."

Bavaro could hardly believe the irony of it all. Brian had always wanted so badly to be one of the guys at the pinnacle of the football world. Now he was about to play in the Super Bowl, and he wanted nothing to do with it.

Leaving the restaurant, all Bavaro could do was tell Brian that he would be thinking of him and praying for him. He certainly could not say what else was running through his mind—the unsettling thought that what had started as a fairy tale might instead be turning into a complete disaster that would end up haunting Brian for the rest of his life. As much as Bavaro wanted to believe that Brian would somehow pull himself together and be able to do his job without ever being noticed, he could not help but think that something bad was going to happen to his friend in the Super Bowl.

The morning of Saturday, January 24, the Patriots had one more practice in Foxborough before they would depart the next day for Houston: one final chance for Brian to get things right and feel good about himself on the way out of town. Instead, he threw two more bad snaps (out of five) during the field-goal period. They were low this time, instead of high. Ken Walter was able to handle them, and Adam Vinatieri still made good on the kicks, but any chance of a boost in Brian's confidence was gone.

It was looking more and more like Brian was suffering from what some athletes, primarily golfers and baseball players, had come to call a case of the yips—an inexplicable loss of ability to do something that had always been so simple for him. One of the greatest golfers of all time, Ben Hogan, had famously gone through multiple stretches when he battled the yips while putting. A baseball pitcher named Steve Blass, winner of two games for the Pittsburgh Pirates in the 1971 World Series and a Major League All-Star in 1972, suffered such a sudden and severe loss of control on his pitches in 1973—with no physical explanation whatsoever—that his ten-year career came crashing to a halt and the baseball version of the yips became commonly known as Steve Blass Disease. Was Brian on his way to having his name forever linked to a football variety of the mysterious mental affliction?

That afternoon, he went to a birthday party for Ken Walter's two-year-old son, Kenny. Although a number of Patriots players were there, it was clearly a time for fun and games and cake, not for football talk. But Brian could not help himself. Sitting with only Walter at one point, he apologized for the way he'd been snapping and then went on and on about the fear and anxiety he was feeling. "You just got to stop worrying so much," Walter said. "Look, I'm a good holder, you know that. Just give me something to catch, just get it in the vicinity, and we'll get it done."

Later, back in his hotel room, alone with his tape recorder, Brian said, "I just want so badly to honor God, and to honor my wife and kids, and my students in the school. I want them to be proud of my performance. So I just need to overcome this and get through it."

Brian reminded himself that he did not need to look to Bill Belichick or Brad Seely for approval. All he needed to do was look to the words of Proverbs 3:5, and he offered his own interpretation out loud: "Trust in the Lord with all your heart and lean not on your own understanding."

Fourteen

A big part of the problem was that Brian simply had too much time on his hands, way too much time to think, and absent any switch to turn off his worrying, he kept seeing in his mind's eye the recurring image of another long snapper named Trey Junkin. Only a year earlier, Junkin had pretty much been Brian, except that he had survived even longer than Brian in the NFL. After nineteen years with five teams—the Buffalo Bills, Washington Redskins, Los Angeles (and Oakland) Raiders, Seattle Seahawks, and Arizona Cardinals—the forty-one-year-old Junkin had finally retired and returned home to Winnfield, Louisiana. Leaving the game had not been easy for Junkin. Sure, he had once expounded for the benefit of NFL Films on the challenges of his job, most notably the concept of routinely getting clobbered on the head by three-hundred-pound men, and he had stared into the camera to pronounce: "Mamas, don't let your babies grow up to do this. Make 'em be doctors." But that was not how he really felt. No matter what he advised others, Junkin was all in when it came to being a snapper. Eleven times he underwent surgery—five times on his left knee alone, plus a variety of cuttings on his shoulders and elbows—but no injury ever stopped him from eventually returning to the field for more beatings. He proudly displayed a tattoo of the NFL logo on his left leg and often wrote poetry about his life in football.

> *Some want this life*
> *Not knowing the cost*
> *Of mind and soul*
> > *So . . .*
> *Do you want a peek*
> *At my world?*
>
> *Dirty jobs . . .*
> *They're all I have*
>
> *Looking back*
> *A different world*
> *Upside down*
> *Very few see it*
> *Three hundred pounders*
> *Breathing hard . . . Mad*
> *Waiting . . . for you to move*
> *The ball*
> *Games inside of Games*
> *This trick*
> *Snapping the ball*
> *Fifteen or eight yards*

It's right there
Or . . . you're gone
No maybe's!
A different world
Looking back . . .

It's a living!

Junkin never stopped working on the mechanics of his craft, and
he never quit obsessing over details. To wit: he always made sure
his fingernails were cut the night before a game. After all, he
would never want the distraction of a ripped nail when a game
was on the line and a football needed to be gripped and delivered.
Back in Winnfield, Junkin sometimes missed the excitement of the
NFL, but he did not miss being hit by oversize linemen or having
to worry about a proper manicure.

Then—after being out of the NFL for the entire 2002 season—
he got an end-of-December phone call from the New York Giants,
who were about to play the San Francisco 49ers in the opening
round of the playoffs. The Giants had struggled all year with their
kicking game, and now their most recent addition as a snapper,
Dan O'Leary, the same Dan O'Leary who would later compete
with Brian at the Patriots tryout, was ruled out with a thumb
injury. Giants head coach Jim Fassel wanted Junkin because they
had been together in Arizona—Fassel as an assistant coach—and
he had great faith in the retired snapper. Junkin saw it as an ideal
opportunity. Days earlier, he had been asked by a local writer to
pick the teams he thought would make it to the upcoming Super

Bowl, and he had named the Giants and the Raiders. That was the only reason he temporarily gave up the deer stands of what he called "backwoods Louisiana" for the bright lights of New York—because he thought he might get an easy ride to the Super Bowl.

Things did not work out quite that gloriously. Playing in San Francisco on January 5, 2003, the Giants held a commanding 38–14 lead late into the third quarter. Then came one of the most remarkable comebacks in league history. The 49ers, led by quarterback Jeff Garcia and wide receiver Terrell Owens, sent the Candlestick Park crowd of 66,318 into a frenzy by scoring twenty-five unanswered points and surging ahead, 39–38, with only 1:05 to play. Still, the Giants had one last chance to pull out a victory. With six seconds left, they lined up for a forty-one-yard field goal. Earlier in the fourth quarter, Junkin had thrown a bad snap that messed up the timing of kicker Matt Bryant and resulted in a critical field-goal attempt sailing wide to the left. This was Junkin's chance to redeem himself. Instead, what happened next was ugly and painful for New York fans, and excruciating for Junkin. He threw a wobbly ball that bounced just in front of holder Matt Allen's outstretched hands. Allen was able to control the ball and stand it on the ground for Bryant. But it was too late. The kicker was totally out of sync and could not regroup. Allen jumped to his feet and yelled the standard call—"Fire! Fire!"—to let his teammates know that the kick was aborted and he would either run or throw the football. Scrambling to his right, Allen heaved the ball downfield, but it landed harmlessly on the ground, dead, same as the Giants' season.

It was the second-largest collapse in NFL playoff history. (In

1993, Houston had been ahead of Buffalo 35–3 before losing in overtime.) No matter how woefully the whole Giants team had fallen apart, though, Junkin took the brunt of the blame. As the father of two boys, both then in their teens, Junkin had always stressed to them the importance of accepting responsibility for their actions, and now it was his turn. Much to his credit, he faced an onslaught of New York and national media types, not exactly the most subtle of creatures, and, with moist, red eyes, he answered their questions as best he could.

"I cost fifty-eight guys a chance to go to the Super Bowl," Junkin said. "My career is over. I'm done. And I'd give anything in the world, except my family, at this point, right now, to have stayed retired."

For nineteen years, hardly anybody even knew his name because he had done his job so well. Now he was going to be all over the New York tabloids—"The Cruel Hands of Fate," the front page of *Newsday* would declare in a bold headline. Junkin quickly became the subject of incessant ranting on talk radio. And the television replays of his nightmarish moment might as well have been running on continuous loop. All of a sudden, everyone was talking about the importance of long snappers. One of the best lines came from Hall of Fame kicker Jan Stenerud, who tried to put into perspective the general indifference toward a snapper until something goes wrong. "It's like a bad intersection," he said. "Most times, there is no stoplight until there's an accident."

A psychologist friend soon told Junkin that he would hurt for ninety days, and then he would feel better. What kind of nonsense was that? Long past the three-month mark, he was still tormented by the snap that got away, still waking up in the middle of the night with a redundant collection of flashbacks and what-ifs. "If I live to be a hundred, it'll happen once a week," Junkin told an interviewer. "It's just something I'm gonna have to live with."

Now Brian was living with it, too. He kept thinking that he might be on the way to doing something that would turn him into another Trey Junkin. Or worse. After all, when Junkin misfired, it cost his team a first-round playoff game. Brian would soon be playing on the grandest of all American sports stages—and with millions upon millions of people watching on television all over the world. The mere thought of messing up in the Super Bowl, of maybe even becoming *the* unforgettable goat of the game, simply horrified him.

Another story from many years earlier—also of a supposedly washed-up long snapper making a late-season return to the NFL— would have been a whole lot better for Brian to dwell on. It was the story of Tom Goode, who spent four years as a top-notch offensive lineman with the Houston Oilers and four with the Miami Dolphins, doubling as a long snapper. Prior to the 1970 season, Goode suffered a bad string of knee and wrist injuries, and the Dolphins placed him on their "injured reserve" list, meaning that they still retained his NFL rights—with certain restrictions—but also that he probably would not play that year. Goode went home to West Point, Mississippi, assuming that his career was over. Then, first week in December, the telephone rang. The Dolphins really needed him and wanted to know if he could make it back. Goode flew to Miami and was in a doctor's office for his physical when everything changed again. The Dolphins had been unable to clear him through the NFL "waiver" system that allowed other teams to claim him before he could return to his old team the same season he'd been put on reserve. If Goode wanted to play football again, he would be doing so with the Baltimore Colts. Worse things could have happened. With quarterback Johnny Unitas leading the way, the Colts were one of the best teams in the league. Goode borrowed a winter coat from a friend and headed north. A month and a half later, on January 17, 1971, he was playing with the Colts in Super Bowl V against the Dallas Cowboys.

That was when Goode's already improbable journey was elevated to the truly remarkable. The score was tied, 13–13, when the Colts made a dramatic last-minute interception that gave them a shot at victory. With nine seconds left, they called time-out and gathered themselves for a thirty-two-yard, game-winning field goal. Only weeks removed from being unemployed and watching the NFL on television from his couch, Goode was about to have the league championship resting in his hands. Of course, holder Earl Morrall and kicker Jim O'Brien would also have a lot to do with the outcome, but only if Goode could first get them the football without incident. Once the Colts were ready for action, the Cowboys called a time-out of their own. They wanted to "ice" the rookie kicker and let the pressure build on him. Goode waited calmly. And he said a prayer. He did not ask for a good snap or for victory. He mainly wanted to express his appreciation for being where he was. *God, thanks. And be with brother Jim, Lord. He's got a big job to do. And Lord, be with the Cowboys, because I think we're going to win this game!*

"It seemed like a week went by during those time-outs," Goode would recall many years later. "But I was just thankful to be there. After all the years I had played, all the balls I had snapped, it was just the ultimate thing, and I was thanking God for putting me in that situation."

The referee eventually blew his whistle for play to resume. The snap and the hold were perfect. The kick was good. And the score was final: 16–13. The Colts were Super Bowl champions. Goode was a Super Bowl champion.

A few days later, he appeared somewhere unthinkable for a long snapper: on the cover of *Sports Illustrated*. Due to the angle of the photo chosen to memorialize the winning kick—it was taken from behind the Dallas defense—Goode was front and center while O'Brien was only partially visible in the background. Of course, the magazine never mentioned Goode in its game story. Why say anything about the snapper when all goes right? But the cover photo alone was more than anything Goode ever could have imagined. It captured him right after unleashing the final snap of his career, forever freezing him in his standard hunched-over position, with Dallas linebacker Chuck Howley using his back as a step stool while trying to block the kick. Years later, *decades* later, people were still mailing copies of that magazine to Goode for him to autograph.

"That one play probably got me more publicity than all the other plays, all the other years, put together," Goode said. "Usually nobody even thinks about the old center until he makes a bad snap. It's a thankless job. But making that one snap, being on the cover of *Sports Illustrated* and all—I guess that was my claim to fame."

In November 2003, the month before Brian got his call from the

Patriots, Goode announced that he was retiring from his second career—a long stretch of coaching college football that included stints as an offensive assistant at four Southeastern Conference schools and concluded with twelve years as head coach at East Mississippi Community College. The Mississippi legislature offered a resolution commending Goode for his many years in athletics, and also for his work with the Enon Baptist Church and a number of civic organizations. Goode was quite certain that he never would have been able to reach and impact young people the way he had without that one high-profile snap of a football in the 1971 Super Bowl.

"I've probably used that story thousands of times," Goode said. "It's meant a lot through the years, especially to young kids. You can get their attention with it. And then you've got a chance to really talk to them."

Yes, Brian would have been infinitely better off flooding his thoughts with the storybook ending of Tom Goode instead of pummeling himself with the cautionary debacle of Trey Junkin. But Brian had never even heard of Goode. And he could not get the specter of Junkin out of his mind.

Fifteen

A white fire engine, lights flashing and siren blaring, led the Patriots' buses out of a parking lot at Gillette Stadium. A few thousand fans waved and cheered, all bundled up against a wind chill of three degrees as they stood behind steel barricades and did the best they could to catch a glimpse of their favorite players. "Dedicated people," Brian said to nobody in particular as he watched out a bus window and waved right back at the frenzied fans. This was early in the afternoon of Sunday, January 25, and the Patriots were on their way to Logan Airport for their flight to Houston and the Super Bowl. Countless additional fans, shivering but nonetheless giddy, lined the sidewalks along U.S. Route 1 and shouted out with love and support. If the treatment the Patriots were now getting was any indication of the week to come, Brian and his teammates were in for quite an experience.

It was not only *playing* in a Super Bowl that would be a first for Brian. The oldest player on the team—the oldest on either team preparing for the game in Houston—had never even been to one. He had been close. Several times he had traveled to Super Bowl cities and participated in NFL-sanctioned events to raise money and awareness for local charities, usually including a food bank, in the days leading up to the game. But he never wanted to stay for the game itself. Brian had always said that the only way he would ever go to a Super Bowl was as a participant. If he was not playing, he was not going. So he would inevitably end up flying home in time to watch on television. Now he could think back to those days and smile about them. He could smile because he had never broken that pact with himself—and he was finally headed to the Super Bowl for more than just pre-game festivities. Going as both a player and a schoolteacher only made it better that it had taken him so long to get there. Because now he was not going as some untouchable gladiator who had nothing in common with any of the regular people who would be watching it all. Strangely enough, he was now pretty much one of them. A thirty-eight-year-old seventh-grade teacher in the Super Bowl? The name on the back of his jersey might as well have been changed to "Everyman." And what a remarkable thing to be: Everyman at the Super Bowl . . . Everyman *playing* in the Super Bowl.

The travel day gave Brian a good opportunity to get away from all the stress he had been feeling, to clear his head and get a fresh start. On the chartered 757 to Houston, he leaned back and watched a movie. After landing at Ellington Field and a bus ride to the Inter-Continental Hotel, where the Patriots would be staying until the night before the game, Brian dropped his luggage in his assigned room and grabbed dinner. Then he took off in a rental car to visit a few old friends. It just so happened that they played for the team that the Patriots would soon be battling for the NFL championship.

The Carolina Panthers had come a mighty long way since Brian played for them in 1999 and 2000. Led by second-year head coach John Fox and newcomer Jake Delhomme at quarterback, they had overcome what Brian playfully called the Kinchen Curse. The year after letting him go, the Panthers had the worst record in football, winning only one of sixteen games, which resulted in the firing of head coach George Seifert. The only other time Brian had been cut by an NFL team, the Green Bay Packers in 1991, his release had also been followed by a disastrous season for the team that let him go (an equally pathetic record of 1–15) and the firing of the head coach (Lindy Infante). Coincidence? Or curse? Brian always got a chuckle out of that. Either way, the Panthers had turned things around in a remarkably short time—from 1–15 in 2001 to a regular-season record of 11–5 in 2003—and now Brian would be playing against the same organization that three years earlier had seemingly put an end to his career. Brian was not thinking in terms of payback—what good would that do?—but he could certainly revel in the delicious irony of the situation.

Carolina had reached the Super Bowl by defeating the Philadelphia Eagles in the NFC championship game. With a good number of former teammates still playing for the Panthers, Brian wanted to visit with them before the week got too busy and the countdown to kickoff might make such socializing a bit awkward. After speaking by phone with tight end Kris Mangum, who was in his seventh year with Carolina, Brian made a half-hour drive to the Wyndham

Greenspoint, where the Panthers were staying, on Houston's northern outskirts. Sitting in the lobby with Mangum and team chaplain Mike Bunkley, sharing both memories and updates, Brian was well situated for brief reunions with a smattering of other guys who happened to pass by and see him. Brian enjoyed spending a few minutes with each of them: defensive end Mike Rucker, defensive backs Mike Minter and Damien Richardson, kicker John Kasay, and others. To each man, Brian offered pretty much the same abbreviated version of the "kind of surreal" circumstances that had delivered him to where he was now sitting.

"Are you going to play anymore after this?" Kasay wanted to know.

"Oh, no, no, no," Brian said, practically recoiling. "Without a doubt, this is it. One more game, and then I'm home with my family."

Kasay had no idea that Brian had been struggling with his snaps. He would hear about that later in the week and immediately make the link to this conversation. He would then understand why Brian had reacted with such certitude that the Super Bowl would be his final game of professional football.

The next afternoon, the Patriots had a light practice at Rice University, and Brian found himself right back in a funk. He had a bunch of good snaps. But he also threw two high balls during the punt period and then a low one that Ken Walter had to trap against the ground while practicing with the field-goal unit. Belichick did not do any yelling this time. But he definitely had Brian on his mind.

Walking slowly off the field at the end of practice, Brian noticed that Belichick seemed to be looking right at him, perhaps trying to catch his attention. He did the best he could to avoid eye contact with his coach. All he wanted to do was get off the field and sidestep any negative rehash of what he already knew to be yet another disappointing practice session. Brian kept walking. But Belichick called out to him.

"Brian."

He was stuck.

Brian stopped, and Belichick walked over to him.

Speaking in a calm and matter-of-fact way, Belichick offered a simple tutorial, with his focus on the punt snapping: "Look, Brian, all you got to do with your snaps is finish your hands through to the target. When you get in trouble, it's because you're stopping your snap short, you're not finishing it. Just make sure you fire your hands to his hip line"—meaning the hip line of the punter—"and the ball will be right where it needs to be. Just think about that follow-through, that finish with your hands, and you'll be fine."

It was nothing Brian had not already known for years, nothing he had not already heard a thousand times as a player and said another thousand times as a coach. But he did not take the comments only at face value. He also processed them as Belichick's way of reaching out with support and saying, "Calm down. I'm still behind you. Everything is going to be okay." Brian would never know if he was reading too much into the brief exchange, but it nonetheless gave him temporary peace.

"Thanks, Bill."

Brian gave his coach a light pat on the stomach and headed for the locker room.

That night, alone in his hotel room, with the door closed and curtains drawn to at least somewhat protect the windows in case of errant fire, Brian spent a few minutes setting up for target practice. He pulled a few pillows from the side-by-side queen-size beds, and he carefully positioned them against the wall just beneath the windows, strategically stacking them and propping them up so that they would stand at attention for him. Then he went for the football and gloves he had surreptitiously packed away and removed from the locker room after practice. Already wearing sweatpants and a T-shirt, Brian pulled on his gloves, and then he was ready. This was how bad things had gotten. Seeking to restore his confidence, Brian was about to go through his motions in a late-night solo session within the cramped confines of an average-size hotel room.

He placed the ball on the floor directly in front of the door. Facing away from the room, he positioned himself over the ball, gripped it, and looked back through his legs at the pillows. He wanted to hit the fluffy target—his imaginary "holder" for a placekick—about a foot and a half to two feet off the ground. Taking in a deep breath, he reminded himself to follow through with his hands, to finish, and then he fired away.

Thwack. Right into the pillows. Precisely where he wanted it. Brian retrieved the ball and did it again. Ten times in a row he threw good balls. Then he took a break and did it again—ten more snaps without a single throw hitting either the curtains or the floor. The football found the carpet only after bouncing off the pillows. After three sets of ten, Brian felt pretty good about himself. He was ready for bed.

The next day, Tuesday, January 27, the annual circus known as Super Bowl media day was held at Reliant Stadium. It was an opportunity for writers and broadcasters from all over the world to ask players and coaches from the Patriots and Panthers—one team at a time—nearly anything they wanted to know. Sometimes the questions would actually have something to do with football, although that was by no means a requirement. With the NFL having issued credentials to more than three thousand journalists—and with the term *journalist* being used quite loosely—there would be no shortage of wacky moments. After all, the whole Super Bowl experience had long since expanded way beyond even the standard excesses of most big-time sporting events. Other than the game itself, the rest of the week was all about hype and entertainment.

The Patriots dressed for media day in the same uniforms—blue jerseys and silver pants—that they would wear for the game. Once they were on the field, the players and coaches adhered to something of a caste system as they positioned themselves for the unleashing of the credentialed masses. Belichick and the most prominent players were each assigned to a podium equipped with a microphone and loudspeakers. Players and assistant coaches considered to be on the next level of status were spread out and given assigned seats in the stands. All the other guys were free to walk around and fend for themselves.

Brian was a walk-around guy. When the journalists entered on the concourse level and he saw how many people were suddenly streaming down through the stands to join the Patriots on the field, his jaw was about ready to hit the ground. "Unbelievable," Brian said to a few teammates who were standing with him on the side-line. "All for a football game, huh?"

Players and coaches were queried about offense and defense and about the personal stories that made them who they were. They were also asked some of the most ridiculous questions imaginable.

"When you wear the helmet, does it mess up your hair? How do you deal with the helmet head?"

"If you could tackle one person, either Clay Aiken or Celine Dion, who would you pick?"

"Can you spell *Massachusetts*? How about *referee*?"

And those were questions from adults. An eleven-year-old girl gathering material for *Weekly Reader,* an educational magazine for students, kept walking around and asking players, "Who on your team can eat the most hot dogs?"

Players with their own video cameras interviewed other players. Local television reporters interviewed national broadcasters. Perhaps the lowlight of the one-hour session with the Patriots came when someone asked safety Rodney Harrison to name the craziest place he had ever "made whoopee" with his wife. Harvey Araton of the *New York Times*—attending his first Super Bowl media day—decided it was "sports journalism's most repellent day of the year."

Brian had his own share of nutty moments. At one point, he was approached by a guy dressed as a superhero: black tights, black mask, orange-and-green cape. He identified himself as Pick Boy, and it turned out that he was from a Nickelodeon cartoon show called *U-Pick Live.* Pick Boy wanted to know if it was true that Brian was the oldest guy on the team, and Brian confirmed that for him. Pick Boy asked, "Are you scared you're going to break a hip?" Brian and a few reporters standing around him all laughed. "Not this Sunday," Brian said. "No hips." He was also asked by someone from *The Tonight Show with Jay Leno* who he thought was better looking—him or Tom Brady? "Unfair question," Brian said.

More than anything, though, Brian was asked—by serious journalists—to tell the story of how he had been called out of the classroom to join the Patriots. He welcomed the opportunity to keep sharing the story because it allowed him to put the focus right where he wanted it: on his faith, on his desire to honor God. Brian kept speaking, and writers kept scribbling. Combine the already unusual existence of a long snapper with the almost absurd circumstances that had landed Brian with the Patriots—his long-ago retirement and year-earlier string of three failed tryouts, his second career as a seventh-grade Bible teacher, and the desperate late-season call from the Patriots—and it was really no wonder that the writers who happened upon Brian ended up wanting every detail they could get out of him.

Trying to put his whole hard-to-believe narrative into perspective, Brian compared it with something out of fiction: "You hear about it. You read about it. You might even see it in a movie. But I don't think you ever expect to be a part of it. What are the odds?" After a while, all he could say was "I've run out of words to describe it." That was not a problem. The writers would have no trouble taking what he had already given them and spicing it up with their own personal touches.

Tampa Tribune columnist Martin Fennelly would introduce readers to Brian by writing, "Meet the newest New England Patriot. Meet the oldest New England Patriot. Meet a story that warms hearts and blesses this game." Gary Shelton of the *St. Petersburg Times* would come up with an equally appropriate way of putting it: "Say hello to the luckiest man in the Super Bowl." After mentioning that Brian had spent part of his fall as a volunteer assistant with Nick Saban and the LSU Tigers, Shelton would also point out that he might be only days away from claiming a spot in football record books: "If LSU rewards Kinchen with a ring, and if the Patriots win the Super Bowl, Kinchen could be the only player in history to win a college championship ring and a Super Bowl ring in less than a month. As miracles go, that's not as good as Jonah and the whale, but it's close." Mike Lopresti of Gannett News Service would also make good use of the Bible-teacher angle. Referring to the first call Brian got from the Patriots during class, and his initial reluctance to accept their invitation to a tryout, Lopresti would write, "God was giving him one more chance. Who says no to God, not to mention Bill Belichick?"

There would be additional stories in a few other newspapers, and they would all make for good reading. But none would include any mention of the most pressing issue Brian was now facing—his inability to snap with any consistency. Some of the stories would report just the opposite. The Lopresti column for Gannett: "His snaps have been straight and true." Sportswriter Sheldon Mickles in the *Baton Rouge Advocate*: "He's been flawless."

Oh, if those writers only knew about the emotional turmoil that was eating up their favorite football-snapping Bible teacher. If they only knew the level of doubt concealed below the surface. That night, Brian once again set up pillows against the wall in his hotel room. And this time he increased the number of snaps. He threw forty instead of thirty.

Sixteen

Concerned about poor conditions of the field they were using for practice at Rice University, the Patriots got permission from the NFL to move their Wednesday-afternoon session indoors to the "bubble" practice facility of the Houston Texans, just across the street from Reliant Stadium. The Patriots would practice there for the rest of the week. The change of scenery did nothing to help Brian. Despite his nocturnal success throwing against pillows in the privacy of his hotel room, he reverted to his struggles once he was back with the team. In fact, not only did he return to the same level of inconsistency at which he had been operating. He took a deep dive from there—ending up with the worst collection of snaps he had ever thrown in a single day.

First, during field-goal period, Brian snapped a ball over Ken Walter's head, and he was immediately thrown right back into what he thought of as "a prison" of fear and doubt. He did not have a clue as to what he could possibly be doing so wrong.

All Brian knew for sure was that he could not figure out how to break free from whatever was keeping him mentally and physically locked up. And this was only the beginning of the nasty descent that would come to define his day.

After the ninety-minute, full-squad practice, Brian, Walter, and Adam Vinatieri went into the stadium, along with special-teams coach Brad Seely, so they could get a feel for the environment. They started with field goals from a variety of distances, about a dozen at each end of the field. One of every three or four snaps was good, but the rest were all over the place. Seely, Walter, and Vinatieri were acutely aware that Brian was in deep trouble, but none of them outwardly expressed a whole lot of emotion about it. This was way too late for any coach or anyone else to get on Brian about his performance. What good would any criticism or even anger do at this point? Plus, nobody could possibly be any harder on Brian than he was already being on himself. "Come on, Brian!" he scolded himself. "What are you *doing*?"

All Walter and Vinatieri could do was just keep plugging away. Working with Brian was still relatively new to Vinatieri; he had never known what it was like to work with him during all those years when Brian was one of the most consistent and respected long snappers in the NFL. For Walter, though, the situation was entirely different. He had known Brian since the early 1990s, when, as a ball boy, he had seen him both snap and play tight end for the Cleveland Browns. Then they had later spent those two years working together as the snapper and the punter/holder for the Carolina Panthers, and they had become good friends. Taking snaps from Brian, Walter had always known him to be a perfectionist who almost never threw anything but an absolute strike. Now this.

Walter told himself that he would just have to "step it up" as a holder in order to overcome Brian's lack of accuracy: *Receivers make a quarterback look good by making good catches. Same thing I need to do for Kinch.* Fortunately for the Patriots, Walter was one of the best holders in the league. He took tremendous pride in his ability to handle just about anything thrown his way, sometimes even going so far as to call himself "the Ozzie Smith of holders"— a reference to the baseball Hall of Famer who was one of the best-fielding shortstops of all time. On the field at Reliant Stadium, Walter was now reaching and stretching so much for Brian's snaps that he would later joke about the workout his abs were getting. But he kept handling the snaps and getting the balls down with a good spot for Vinatieri, and the kicker kept booming them through the uprights. Of course, the final outcome of each kick did nothing to ease either the frustration or the worry that kept assaulting Brian's nerves.

Seely finally suggested it was time to move from field goals to punting. Perhaps the change would somehow help Brian. It did not. His first snap bounced in front of Walter. Seely told his punter to move up a yard or two. Maybe that would enable Brian to get in a groove, and then they could move back to the regular distance of fifteen yards. This was new territory for the special-teams coach, and he was willing to try almost anything. Brian managed to improve his punt snaps after that, but he still failed to find the consistency he wanted and needed.

When they were done in the stadium, Walter and Vinatieri walked off together, just the two of them, and when they looked at each other, Walter could almost see in Vinatieri's eyes the same unspoken questions he was asking himself: *What do we do? How do we handle this?* Walter suggested that they might want to slow down a little bit on field goals. Maybe Vinatieri ought to wait a moment or two longer than normal before starting his approach to the ball, which would allow Walter extra time to handle whatever Brian sent their way. "Just wait till the ball gets to the spot, and then go," Walter said. "We'll be a little slower than usual, but we'll get it done." Walter and Vinatieri also reminded each other of a general rule they had put in place long before Brian joined the team: if a ball ever gets away from them, Walter would be the one to chase it down and pick it up, not Vinatieri. Even with such a negative thought in mind, though, they both kept telling themselves that everything would be all right. "Look, I know I have the best holder," Vinatieri said. "We just need to let Brian get through this the best he can. We'll be okay."

Meanwhile, Brian walked alone off the field, deeply upset about the position in which he was putting his teammates and coaches. They had worked way too hard and accomplished way too much for one person—for him—to somehow blow the whole season for them. But he was single-handedly putting them all at risk. What should he do about it? What *could* he do about it?

Brian went by himself to lift weights. And to think.

When he finally got back to the hotel, at almost seven o'clock, he had a quick dinner and then went to find Brad Seely. Brian wanted to look at the videotape from practice and try to figure out what he was doing wrong. He and Seely came up with one possibility. Brian had always focused on keeping his back as straight as he could—almost parallel to the ground—when snapping. On the tape, his upper back and shoulders appeared to be pointing down too much when he released the football, creating angles that increased the likelihood of a high snap. But what about the balls Brian had bounced on the ground? Were they the result of over-compensating for a high one? No matter how many times Brian and Seely ran the tape in slow motion, they were unable to pinpoint anything definitive about Brian's mechanics that would explain his alarming inconsistency. That was the hardest part of the whole thing. If Brian could just figure out what in the heck he was doing wrong, he could fix it.

By the time Brian left Seely, the intense frustration of the moment, combined with all the pressure Brian had already been feeling, was about to break him. This was no longer just about getting a football where it needed to be. This was about being on the verge of blowing up on the biggest sports stage in America—and with enough cameras in place to capture a multitude of angles for posterity.

Brian wrestled with what he knew to be a mighty contradiction. On one hand, he was simply getting ready to play a football game. A *game*. How could anything that happened in a football game possibly matter in the grand scheme of things? He kept reminding himself that it would never make a difference in the eyes of God. On the other hand, Brian was nonetheless feeling overwhelmed by the prospect of costing his team a championship and looking like a total buffoon for all the world to see and ridicule. No, *ridicule* did not even cover it. How about *hate* and *scorn*? After all, many of the same New Englanders now reveling in the great success of the Patriots already had a track record that illustrated how they were likely to respond to a critical miscue by one of their own. Most of them had never managed to find any warmth in their hearts for the man they blamed for costing their beloved Boston Red Sox the 1986 World Series. More than seventeen years later, fans and the media still disdained first baseman Bill Buckner for the slow grounder, hit by Mookie Wilson of the New York Mets, that rolled through his legs and allowed the winning run in Game 6. Cruel jokes still circulated: *Hey, did you hear Buckner tried to commit suicide? He jumped in front of a bus, but it went between his legs.* Stories were still written about "the Buckner game," and they sometimes included people recalling where they had been when "it" happened, as if President Kennedy had been shot again.

Brian fully understood the potential magnitude of what he was getting into. He went to his hotel room, feeling very alone and extremely anxious, and made a decision. All he had to do now was inform Scott Pioli of it. Brian checked his team-issued list of room assignments and dialed the telephone. He did not really expect to find Pioli in his room—calling his cell phone would be next—but Pioli answered.

"Hey, Brian, what's going on?" he casually asked. There was nothing unusual about his old friend just checking in with him. Of course, Pioli had no idea what he was about to hear.

"Scott, I don't know how to say this, but I want to go home. You need to find somebody else to snap."

With the Super Bowl only four days away, Pioli would have been hard-pressed to imagine a player—any player—offering him a more bizarre or more jarring collection of syllables. He knew that Brian had been having problems. But he could not believe that he actually wanted out altogether.

"What are you talking about?" Pioli said.

"I can't throw the football straight," Brian said. "I don't know what I'm doing wrong. I don't understand it. Don't have any idea how to explain it. But this is a nightmare. I'm totally lost."

Pioli did the best he could to play down the situation. He tried to reassure Brian that he would be fine. He had been snapping forever. Everything would work itself out.

"Scott, are you kidding me?" Brian said. "Where have you been? I'm throwing balls over Kenny's head. I'm throwing balls on the ground."

"You'll be fine," Pioli said. "The whole reason we brought you in is because we know what you can do. The biggest thing is you just need to trust yourself—not only now, not only with snapping or anything else related to football. It's everything. It's always. It's *life*."

That was one thing about the relationship between Pioli and Brian. They had been friends for so long that Pioli knew exactly what existed behind the mask of certainty that Brian generally wore for everyone other than the people closest to him. Pioli knew that a great deal of insecurity had always lurked behind the mask, and it was this understanding that now allowed him to go much deeper with Brian than a typical front-office guy could have done with a player who was not also a friend. Pioli and Brian went back and forth for a few minutes on that subject of trusting and believing in yourself.

Then Brian asked about something that seemed quite strange to Pioli. He wanted to know why Belichick had not been yelling at him when he messed up.

"Why doesn't Bill curse me out?" Brian said. "Why isn't he 'mother-effing' me like he does to everyone else? He certainly used to in Cleveland. And I deserve it."

"Who knows?" Pioli said. "Maybe he knows your confidence is already down, and he doesn't want to make it worse."

Pioli was by no means a psychologist. But this was starting to feel an awful lot like trying to talk down someone who was about to jump from a ledge.

"Brian, you just need to start thinking clearly about this," Pioli said. "You're not going anywhere. You're not going home. You're *in*. You committed to this thing. You've got to think about the commitment you made to Bill and to me, and to all the people here."

"Yeah, I've made a commitment. But what is that worth if all I'm gonna do is screw up this whole thing for so many people?"

Brian paused. Then he said, "I really feel like I need to talk to Bill."

"I don't understand," Pioli said. "What is that going to accomplish?"

Ultimately, Brian decided not to bother Belichick. Pioli had done a pretty good job of calming down his friend. And Brian finally agreed that he was not going anywhere. He would just keep plugging away and would do the best he could to get everything back to normal.

After hanging up the phone, Pioli took in a deep breath and just sat there for a minute. Although he had already known Brian was not throwing great snaps, this was the first time he was genuinely concerned about it. With Brian revealing such a lack of confidence, how could he not be? Pioli knew he would have to tell Belichick what had just taken place.

Brian was temporarily comforted by his conversation with Pioli. If nothing else, it felt good to know that he was still wanted. But Brian soon got antsy again, his brain stuck in overthink, and he decided to go see Don Davis, his teammate and friend who led the Patriots' weekly Bible study. Although Davis was only in his first season with New England, he already knew something about the whole Super Bowl experience. Two years earlier, when he was with the St. Louis Rams, he had played in Super Bowl XXXVI *against* the Patriots. Brian now went to see Davis in his room because he still needed a friend—in this case, a like-minded co-worker—to hear him out and offer some kind of encouragement.

"I'm really struggling," Brian told Davis.

He explained that he was filled with anxiety, that he could not stop thinking about messing up in the Super Bowl and blowing the game for everyone on the team, that he could hardly even sleep. Brian told him about the conversation with Pioli but said he still could not shake the big-picture questions that had been hanging over him: "Is this really where I'm supposed to be? Is this really what I'm supposed to be doing?"

Davis strongly believed that it was.

"With this incredible opportunity you have been given, with the whole timing of it all, it has to be a God thing," he said. "You were not brought in for training camp. You were not brought in for the whole season. You were brought here for a specific time and purpose. You're right where you're supposed to be. I mean, there are always going to be some problems along the way, but that's just part of the whole process."

Davis had focused on that very concept in a Bible study—"Five Ways God Uses Problems"—he had recently prepared for his weekly session with teammates. Using passages from five different books of the Bible, Davis had illustrated that God uses problems to direct us, to inspect us, to correct us, to protect us, and to perfect us. As Davis had put it in his opening comments: "The problems we face will either defeat us or develop us. Unfortunately, most folks fail to see how God wants to use problems for good in their lives. Most of the time, we react foolishly and resent our problems rather than pausing to consider what benefit they might bring."

The keys for Brian now, Davis told him in that hotel room, would be the same as they always had been: faith and perseverance. "We're going to win the Super Bowl," Davis said. "We're not going to allow the devil to take your confidence, cost us the Super Bowl, and take away this tremendous platform for God." Brian listened intently, and he greatly appreciated the heartfelt support of his new friend.

"Let me pray for you," Davis said.

He and Brian held hands and bowed their heads.

"Thank you, God, for your provision, for your power," Davis said. "We come to you together because where two or more are gathered, you are with us in our midst. Whatever we ask, if we ask in faith, according to your will, we know we will have what we ask for. Our request is that you would fill Brian with your spirit, give him the confidence to do his job, for your glory. We come against the devil right now, in the name of Jesus. The devil is a liar, a thief who wants to steal this glory from you."

Then Davis directly targeted the devil on behalf of Brian: "Devil, you have no authority over this man."

"Amen," Brian said. He did not really believe that any evil force would ever affect his performance on a football field. But he appreciated the kindness and support that Davis offered—and Brian was open to just about anything that might help.

When he returned to his room, Brian took his daily snaps into the pillows. Soon after that, he got a call from Anthony Pleasant, one of his old friends from the Cleveland Browns who was now a veteran defensive lineman for the Patriots. Up to this point, almost every time Pleasant had seen or called Brian in Houston, he had gone right at him with a big smile and a standard line of teasing: "It's all gonna come down to you, Brian. Whole game's gonna be on you, baby." It was the kind of jocular jab that only a good friend would even consider delivering. Pleasant was just trying to lighten the heavy load he knew his friend was carrying. Brian really had no choice but to laugh along with his buddy. But he also transitioned pretty quickly into firm protest: "Man, I hope not. You really need to stop saying that."

This time, Pleasant was not calling to be funny. The man his teammates sometimes called Moses—Pleasant often talked of becoming a minister—wanted to offer his support in more genuine fashion. Knowing what a rough day Brian had been through, he wanted to fill his head with something positive before he went to sleep. Pleasant told Brian, "God did not bring you this far to have you mess up now."

With that thought firmly in mind, Brian repeating it to himself several times after hanging up the phone, he came to a conclusion of his own: *Four more days. I just have to get the job done.*

When he called Lori to talk through the events of the day—and to say good night—she could hardly believe what he had told Pioli about wanting to leave the team. "Have you lost your mind?" Lori said. "You're going to give these people a heart attack. You just need to calm down. Everything's going to be okay."

Lori and the boys would be driving to Houston the next day. Brian already knew that. But just hearing it again from his wife was the best thing he had heard all day. Shortly after eleven o'clock, he told Lori that he loved her, hung up the phone, and turned out the lights on the longest day of his career.

Brian did not know whether Pioli told Belichick about their telephone conversation. But one minor gesture made him wonder. It came during practice the afternoon of Thursday, January 29, less than twenty-four hours after Brian had frantically talked about leaving the team and going home.

After throwing his first punt snap of the day and running downfield on coverage, Brian was headed back to do it again when Belichick looked over at him, put together the tips of his right thumb and index finger, and flashed him the okay sign. Clearly, Belichick wanted Brian to know that he had noticed the good snap. Was he just randomly taking a moment to show approval to his snapper—not exactly a common occurrence—or was he intentionally trying to salvage the spirits of someone he knew to be in desperate need of encouragement? Either way, Brian was indeed lifted, and soon thereafter he was equally pleased when both Ken Walter and Adam Vinatieri complimented him on how well he had snapped throughout the practice.

It was a sweet reprieve. And the timing could not have been better. Brian's family was scheduled to arrive in Houston while he was at practice—and now he could enjoy their time together without being totally preoccupied by all the stress he had been feeling.

Brian was so happy to see them all when he got back to the hotel: Lori; Austin; Hunter; Logan; McKane; and his mother, Toni, unmistakably radiating the happy smile of an extremely excited and proud mom. His father, Gus, and brother Todd would later be arriving from Dallas, where they were attending an event put on by the Fellowship of Christian Athletes. The Kinchens had a big night ahead of them. They were going to NASA's Johnson Space Center for a huge party—more than a thousand people including a bunch of astronauts—in honor of the Patriots and their families.

For Brian, it was one of the best experiences of the whole week. He walked with his boys through the front end of a space shuttle. He watched his sons put on headsets and enjoy an exhibit area known as Mission Kidtrol. And he went with them into a simulator that made them feel like they were traveling in a spaceship. Forget football. This was family. All the Kinchens had a great time.

So much for the reprieve. Brian threw a few more shaky snaps at practice Friday, and Belichick responded to a low one by yelling, "Get it up!"

After practice, Brian took his helmet and shoulder pads back to the team hotel with him—his family was staying elsewhere—and went right to work throwing his ball into the pillows. It was the first time he had done so while wearing his helmet and pads. The idea was to mimic as best he could the way his body would feel during the game, complete with the weight and restrictions of his gear. He took forty snaps.

When he was done, Brian cleaned up both himself and the room. Then he pulled out the same book he had been reading every now and then, *The Man in the Mirror,* and skipped ahead to a chapter that could not have been more relevant. Chapter 17 carried a one-word title: "Fear." On the third page, Brian found a passage that summarized the only thing he needed to know: "To be afraid is to not *fully* trust God. He instructs us not to be afraid, promising that if we cast our anxiety upon Him, He will take care of us." At the end of the chapter, Brian read through a set of focus questions, and one of them might as well have been written directly for him at this very moment: "When you have done everything you can do, and things still don't seem to be working out, how are you to respond?" Brian knew that the answer came in one simple but profoundly powerful word: *faith*. And now—no matter what might happen in the next two days—he needed to keep reminding himself of that.

Back at school in Baton Rouge, the mood was considerably lighter. The students at Parkview had no idea how bad things had gotten for their favorite football player, and their excitement was only building in anticipation of the Super Bowl that weekend. They had even been allowed to put away their school uniforms for the day and wear anything red, white, and blue, in honor of Brian and the Patriots.

Brian would have loved to see all those kids running around in his team colors. Thinking about his students, he decided to make one last videotape for them: a collection of advice from Patriots players and staff. The next day, Saturday, January 31, he found the perfect time to collect material for it. It was the day before the Super Bowl, and the Patriots were in Reliant Stadium for a final walk-through. With the players dressed in their game uniforms, they also posed for official team photos. While everyone was out on the field, Brian walked around with his camera and solicited "words of wisdom" and "life lessons" for his seventh graders.

Some of the players spoke with absolute sincerity and offered exactly the type of messages any teacher or parent would want a big-time professional athlete to share with twelve- and thirteen-year-olds. Tom Brady looked straight into the camera, those piercing blue eyes locked in for the students of Parkview, and said, "Always believe in yourself. No matter what anyone else ever says, the only thing you control is what you can do about yourselves. The harder you work and the more you believe in yourself, the more successful you're going to be." Don Davis said, "Life is all about balance . . . and humility. You can't be too up when the highs come. And you can't be too low when the lows come. It's all about balance."

Of course, football players being football players, Brian also captured a generous sampling of irreverence. *Oh, sure, wisdom or a life lesson? Yeah, I'll give you something to live by.* Defensive lineman Rick Lyle said, "Play golf. Don't play football." One of his colleagues on the defensive line, rookie Dan Klecko, breathlessly instructed, "If you make it here, remember your camera. Don't forget your camera. That's what I did. That's your words of wisdom." But two guys who played on the other side of the ball, offensive linemen Matt Light and Dan Koppen, easily claimed the top prizes for messages the seventh graders least needed to hear. With arms crossed over his number seventy-two jersey and an up-to-no-good look filling every inch between his red mop of hair and an equally unruly goatee, the six-foot-four, three-hundred-pound Light offered only a single line of advice: "Don't listen to your teacher." After hearing that and then allowing himself a good ten seconds for deep thinking, Koppen took the bar even lower when he blurted out this priceless gem: "Don't break through the toilet paper!" Koppen's fellow offensive linemen—standing side by side with him for a group photo—reacted as if it were just about the funniest thing they had ever heard. Brian laughed, too.

All yuks aside, there was one brief comment that would stand above all others as the most memorable—and the most important—for Brian. It came from Scott Pioli, who fully understood that Brian wanted something for his students but instead chose to aim his message directly at the man behind the camera. He wanted Brian to always keep in mind something they had talked about during their intense telephone call three days earlier—the part about Brian having to trust himself. The way Pioli saw it, what he wanted to say now was not just for the video. It was not only for the game the next day. It was for *life*. All he said into the camera was "Remember the conversation." Brian's response was equally short and to the point: "Good one. I like it. Excellent."

Seventeen

Brian had long ago learned not to get too hyped up the day of a game until it was actually time to run out on the field. Why burn precious energy on mental stress when he would soon need all the fuel he could possibly summon for physical combat? Granted, a certain amount of what he termed "nervous expectation" could never be altogether avoided in the hours leading up to kickoff. But he always tried to conserve his energy by not dwelling on such thoughts. In that respect, Brian began the morning of February 1, 2004, Super Bowl Sunday, the same way he had approached the start of any other game day: locked in what he called "conservation mode." Given the level of anxiety he had experienced throughout the week leading up to this, he was both surprised and pleased by how well he had slept the night before the biggest one-day sporting event in the world. Seeking a more controlled and isolated setting, the Patriots had moved into a different hotel—the Houston Hobby

Airport Marriott—for Saturday night. Now Brian was doing the best he could to keep his thoughts and emotions in check.

Alone in his room, Brian prayed, and his big-picture requests were pretty much the same as always. He asked for the strength to give his best in every situation to glorify God. And he asked for faith that would be strong enough to endure whatever events and outcomes God might set before him. Brian also had a specific request that would be quite strange for just about any other professional athlete—other than another long snapper—preparing to play in a game of such magnitude. He prayed that God would allow him to get through it "unnoticed and unmentioned."

Late in the morning, Brian still felt fairly relaxed when he entered a hotel meeting room for the Patriots' pre-game meal. The players had been told to get plenty of food from the buffet because the gap between eating and playing would be considerably longer than usual. Kickoff would not be until 5:25 P.M., but with all the special festivities and pre-game entertainment that are part of a Super Bowl, both teams had to allow for extra time at the stadium. With that in mind, Brian filled his plate and joined a few other players at a round banquet table. All he wanted to do was eat and pass the time.

Yet sometimes the simplest of choices can dramatically alter the course of events.

Brian wanted to cut open and butter a dinner roll. But the crust was rock hard. The dull blade of a butter knife had no chance. Clutching the roll in his right hand—his lead hand for gripping and snapping a football—Brian secured a steak knife in his left hand and went to work. Not a good idea. In the first stroke of what was intended to be a measured sawing motion, the knife cut clear through the roll and sliced deep into Brian's right index finger.

"Gosh *dang* it," he exclaimed.

Brian threw down the knife, and his eyes went straight to the damage. A flap of skin was left exposed on the inside of his finger at the middle knuckle. Blood spilled, and the pain was palpable. More than anything, though, he felt waves of panic and disbelief. How in the world could this happen at a time like this? How would it affect him for the game? "*Crap,*" Brian said. He was fuming. He covered his hand with a napkin and applied pressure to the wound.

The other guys at the table had no idea why he was so agitated.

"What's the problem?" said Larry Izzo, captain of special teams for the Patriots, sitting just to the right of Brian.

"Dude, I just cut my finger really bad."

"You serious?"

"Yeah."

"Let's see what it looks like."

Brian grimaced as he offered his bloody digit for viewing and explained what had happened. Izzo and Mike Vrabel—another linebacker sitting at the table—could not help themselves. They started cracking up. They laughed because they thought it was so ridiculous that a big, strong football player—that anyone—would hurt himself trying to butter a roll. What a goofball!

Brian was not amused. "What's so funny?" he demanded.

"Well, I mean, come on," Izzo said. "Hours from the start of the Super Bowl and our only snapper slices open his finger? Got to admit, that's kind of funny."

"Yeah, for you, maybe."

Izzo and Vrabel chose not to dwell on how this might affect Brian if he had to use that hand to grip and snap a football at a critical moment with the whole season weighing in the balance. Brian could not help but imagine the worst.

A trainer covered the wound with a small bandage—that would suffice for the time being—and instructed Brian to see a team doctor once he got to the stadium. So much for conservation mode. In addition to the lack of confidence that had already afflicted him for weeks, Brian now had a new source of stress to take with him into the biggest game of his life.

He had to scrap his standard routine. Instead of waiting for the last team bus to the stadium, Brian had to take the first, so that he could have a doctor look at his finger. By 12:15, Brian was at his stall in a far back corner of the locker room. Soon thereafter, it was determined that his cut would require stitches, but Brian was concerned that being sewn up might hinder his ability to grip the ball, and the doctor agreed to wait until after the game. For now, he would just tightly bandage the finger to protect it and to keep it from bleeding. Brian was fine with that. He had other things on his mind.

Stuck in the locker room with more time than usual to kill, and really nothing to do but sit and think, Brian did the best he could to focus on a basic set of reminders: *Relax and release. Hands to the target. All the way through to the target. You cannot be tentative. Just fire it back there.* Simple enough. But other thoughts crept in as well. Brian began to torment himself with a whole array of painful possibilities. Among the worst: lining up for a field goal, sailing the ball over Ken Walter's head, and watching the Panthers scoop it up and take it in for a score of their own. This was not exactly an advertisement for the power of positive thinking. But Brian had already been through so much in such a short period of time, and Norman Vincent Peale he was not.

Brian came to two conclusions: One, this was the most nervous he had ever been before a game. Two, he had to prepare himself for the reality that something bad might happen. It was a very real possibility, and he felt that he had to come to peace with that. In the silence of his mind, Brian said, "God, whatever it is you have planned for me, it's going to be okay. I'm just asking you to give me the strength to do my job the best I can. And if you see what I envision, that snap over the holder's head and the Panthers scoring, then I'll just have to be okay with that. I am totally committed to whatever you see."

When Brian finally took the field to warm up with Ken Walter and Adam Vinatieri, he experienced what he would later call the "worst pre-game" of his life. The bandaged finger—further protected by a glove—was not a problem. It was Brian's wounded psyche that was doing the damage. "I've never been more nervous in a football uniform," he would later say into his tape recorder. "I was so nervous, I could barely snap the football. A lot of my short snaps were on the ground, and even my punt snaps were that way, too. I just had no confidence going into the game."

The relentless anxiety kept a firm grip on Brian, and it eventually caused him to do something he had never done. His entire career, he had never prayed about touchdowns, or about victories,

or about anything else so directly related to performance and outcome. But now he was ready to cut a deal. "Give me this one victory
by about three touchdowns," Brian said. "Give me a blowout like
that, and I'll never again ask for anything else."

The excitement of the day was building for the 71,525 people
who had been fortunate enough to secure a ticket into the stadium.
Broadcast crews from all over the world were readying themselves
for a game that would be televised in 229 countries. And Brian was
such a wreck that he was trying to cut a deal with his Maker. He
had been dreaming for so many years about going to a Super Bowl,
about getting to play in one, but the vision had never looked or felt
anything like this. Simply put, the oldest guy in the game had no
idea whatsoever how to handle the daunting reality with which he
was now being confronted.

As the game was about to begin—the Patriots were lining up for
the opening kickoff to the Panthers—Brian stood on the sideline
and tried to convince himself that everything would be okay if
he could somehow just relax and allow his thoughts to stay in the
moment. *I've got to stop thinking about everything that's already happened,* he told himself. *Got to stop imagining what might be coming
next.*

Las Vegas oddsmakers had the Patriots beating the Panthers
by seven points. Pundits had predicted a low-scoring game domi-
nated by the defenses of both teams—with many of the experts
even suggesting that the matchup would make for a relatively dull
Super Bowl. The early going did nothing to dispute that. In fact,
the Patriots and Panthers opened the game without scoring on

eleven straight possessions. It was the longest stretch of scoreless football—twenty-six minutes, fifty-five seconds—in Super Bowl history. What might have been somewhat boring for fans, though, could only be described as deeply frustrating and even alarming for Brian and his fellow New England special teamers.

On their first possession, the Patriots reached the Carolina thirteen-yard line before stalling out and lining up for a thirty-one-yard field-goal attempt. Panthers special-teams coach Scott O'Brien had no idea that Brian had been struggling with his snaps. But having worked with Brian for ten years, a decade of NFL seasons with Cleveland, Baltimore, and Carolina, he certainly knew everything there was to know about his tendencies. O'Brien always tried to give his players an edge by studying film and picking up "keys" that would tip them off to the timing of a snap. Some guys lifted their heels right before snapping, some bowed out their knees, others slightly dropped their rear ends. But O'Brien knew that Brian did nothing of the sort, so he had repeatedly told his players, "Just concentrate on the football. It's going to be the first thing that moves." As far as the Panthers' strategy for blocking a field-goal attempt, the whole idea was to focus on the inside of the line in an area known as the "A" gap between the center (Brian) and the left guard (Wilbert Brown). By breaking down the inside of the line and creating a seam, O'Brien felt that the Panthers could pressure Adam Vinatieri and maybe even get a hand on the ball. Of course, with everything else Brian had on his mind, Carolina's strategy was not an issue to him. All he cared about was getting the ball back—cleanly—to Ken Walter. *Finish with your hands. Straight back to Kenny.*

Brian's snap and Walter's hold were both good. Brian and his line mates blocked the inside charge of the Panthers without any problem. But Vinatieri did something that was extremely unusual for him to do in a big game. He simply made a bad kick, the ball sailing off wide to the right. Vinatieri would take full responsibility, saying he had probably been a little too excited and too fast for his own good. No matter what caused the miss, the New England field-goal unit was clearly off to a less-than-ideal start.

A few minutes later, after a Carolina possession that quickly went nowhere and a similarly futile New England attempt to move the ball, Brian made his first punt snap of the game. The snap was on target, and Walter got off a forty-four-yard punt with no return. Brian was able to exhale as he returned to safety on the sideline. But trouble soon returned. With 3:12 left in the first quarter and the Patriots again punting, this time with Walter standing on the New England forty-five-yard line, Brian bounced the snap more than a yard in front of him. Walter was able to handle it—"a great recovery," announcer Dick Stockton told countless millions on the primary international broadcast of the game—and the Patriots escaped from the play unscathed. In fact, after the pickup by Walter, a well-placed punt, and a fair catch by Steve Smith, the Panthers would have to start from back at their eight-yard line. But a fortunate outcome for the Patriots did nothing to ameliorate the fact that Brian had thrown a bad ball. Watching from upstairs in the New England coaches' booth, Scott Pioli said only two words to himself: *Oh, boy.* But he still somehow thought that everything was going to work out okay.

Early in the second quarter, with the game still scoreless, Brian had to snap for another punt. He was extremely relieved to throw a good one. But he had never before felt such heightened emotions— first total anxiety, then that rush of relief—right before and after performing his job. How many more snaps would he have to survive? When would the Patriots start building a lead that might allow him to stop stressing so much?

With 6:08 left in the second quarter, the Patriots had another good chance to put the first points on the scoreboard. This time they would try to make a field goal from thirty-six yards out. Again, Brian's snap and Walter's hold were good. But this time Scott O'Brien's plan—loading up the middle and trying to collapse the interior left side of the New England line—worked to perfection for the Panthers. Brian held up fairly well against the surge, but left guard Wilbert Brown and left tackle Russ Hochstein were knocked right on their backs, which allowed two Carolina linemen to freely extend their arms skyward and get a good shot at a block. Sure enough, the trajectory of Vinatieri's kick was lower than he would have liked, and defensive tackle Shane Burton got a hand on the ball, which bounced harmlessly away and ultimately rolled dead in the end zone.

What a lousy start for the New England special teams. One field goal missed for no good reason. One punt snap bounced on the ground. A second field goal blocked. And there was still more drama to come.

The scoring drought finally ended when Tom Brady connected with wide receiver Deion Branch on a five-yard touchdown pass with 3:05 left in the half. Then Brian threw a low snap on the extra point. Walter was able to trap and control the ball, and Vinatieri still made the kick, giving the Patriots a 7–0 lead. But the tension continued to mount for the kicking unit. After watching the ball split the uprights, Vinatieri immediately turned to Walter, and they slapped hands, both of them thankful that they had just dodged a bullet.

Back on the sideline, Brian approached his old friend Anthony Pleasant, the big defensive lineman who had taunted him all week about the whole Super Bowl coming down to him having to make a good snap with everything on the line. Pleasant was not playing against the Panthers. He had been declared inactive. (Eight of a team's fifty-three roster players had to be inactive for each NFL game.) But he was nonetheless locked in on everything that was happening with his team . . . and was keenly aware that Brian needed some support.

"I don't know if I can do this," Brian said.

"You don't have a choice," Pleasant responded. "You can do it. You have to." And then—amazingly enough for a time like this— he went right back to the same thing he had been telling Brian all week. But this time Pleasant was not teasing. Looking Brian straight in the eye and speaking with all sincerity, he calmly said, "The game is on you."

"Why are you telling me that?" Brian said.

"Because it is. It's gonna be on you."

Pleasant had known Brian long enough to be fully aware that nothing ever got him going more than a direct challenge. He was just attempting to motivate his friend, trying to push the right button so—as Pleasant would later say—the cream would some- how rise to the top.

The Panthers evened the score with an eight-play, ninety-five-yard drive that ended with Jake Delhomme hitting wide receiver Steve Smith on a thirty-nine-yard touchdown pass. Less than a minute after that, with only eighteen seconds remaining in the first half, the Patriots were right back in the end zone on a five-yard Brady touchdown pass to wide receiver David Givens. So much for the early domination by the defenses. And so much for Brian's hope to stay hidden on the sideline.

Since joining the Patriots, Brian had been called upon to snap no more than nine times in a game. Now, on the one day he most wanted to remain invisible, he was back on the field for the seventh time in the first half alone. And snap number seven was even worse than the previous one. Brian bounced the ball on the ground this time. Walter once again made a nice save for him and managed to put down a good placement for Vinatieri. The kick was good—putting the Patriots back in front by a score of 14–7—but how many more times could Walter keep covering for Brian? How many more times before an errant snap would result in something really bad for the Patriots?

Returning to the sideline, Brian saw Belichick coming after him, and he turned away to avoid the wrath of his coach, walking off to the right. But Belichick kept coming.

"What are you doing, Brian? We need better than that out of you. This is the Super Bowl!"

"I know that."

"Well, you got to get the damn ball back there. You got to get it done."

"I'll get it done," Brian said. "Don't worry about it, I'll get it done."

As Belichick walked away, Brian looked at him and thought something he never would have said out loud to his coach: *You're the one who wanted me here. I didn't ask for any of this.*

The half soon ended with one more score, a last-second, fifty-yard field goal by Carolina kicker John Kasay that cut the Patriots' lead to 14–10. What a turnaround in the overall flow of the game: after almost twenty-seven minutes without anyone scoring, the teams had combined for an outburst of twenty-four points in slightly more than three minutes.

For fans both in the stadium and watching on televisions all over the world, the halftime entertainment would provide one of the most talked-about moments in the history of the much-celebrated Super Bowl halftime show. Pop singers Janet Jackson and Justin Timberlake were not exactly restrained in terms of sexual suggestiveness throughout their performance of "Rock Your Body," which includes the line "Better have you naked by the end of this song." Then they went for pure shock value. Timberlake tugged at the top of Jackson's costume, and the next thing millions of viewers knew, they were being flashed by her right breast. "Wardrobe malfunction," Timberlake would subsequently claim to almost universal ridicule.

While Jackson and Timberlake were gyrating and gesticulating, Brian—oblivious to anything happening outside the Patriots' locker room—was sitting and stewing. And he was wondering why. Why could he not compose himself out on the field? Why could he no longer perform with any consistency a never-changing physical task that had always come so easily to him? And then there was the biggest *why* question of all, the same one he had already asked numerous times during the first half: "Father, why are you doing this to me?"

In the third quarter, the game looked a lot like the opening minutes again—not much offense and a whole lot of defense. The Patriots punted twice in the quarter, and Brian was very pleased to throw two good snaps. He was also able to hustle downfield and get involved at the end of both plays. The first punt hit the ground without the Panthers fielding it, and it took a bad bounce for the Patriots, back toward the line of scrimmage, after which Brian downed the ball at the Carolina forty-two-yard line. It was not too often that the same guy who started a play by snapping the ball also ended up collecting it downfield, an oddity that Brian enjoyed. The second punt actually gave him an opportunity to reverse the usual direction of punishment for a long snapper. Instead of the normal routine of being clobbered by very large men, he was finally able to *make* a hit, lowering his right shoulder and assisting teammate Je'Rod Cherry on the tackle of return man Steve Smith at the Carolina twenty-yard line. It was the first time since joining the Patriots that Brian had gotten in on a tackle, and it felt good. Perhaps the tide had turned for him.

The third quarter ended with Brian having made a total of nine snaps. He was never going to make a highlight film out of them. But he had at least survived three-fourths of the game without doing anything that ended up hurting his team. Now all he needed was more points for the Patriots. At 14–10 with only a quarter left to play, the score was still too close for comfort. The absolute worst scenario Brian ever could have imagined—an undecided game with time running down and the Patriots needing a field goal—still remained a very real possibility. One thought kept flooding his mind: *Come on, guys, let's put this thing away.*

On the second play of the fourth quarter, New England running back Antowain Smith scored on a two-yard touchdown run—and Brian's snap and the extra point were good—to give the Patriots the biggest lead of the game at 21–10. But the Panthers stormed right back with a touchdown on a thirty-three-yard run by DeShaun Foster. Trailing by five points, they went for a two-point conversion that would have put them within a field goal of the Patriots. The attempt failed, and the score remained the same, 21–16. Not for long, though. The next time the Panthers got the ball, deep in their own territory, wide receiver Muhsin Muhammad got behind the New England secondary, and Jake Delhomme unleashed what turned into an eighty-five-yard bomb for both a touchdown and the first Carolina lead of the day. The Panthers again went for two points, and again failed to convert, so the score was 22–21 with 6:53 left to play.

It was the first time since November 23, ten weeks earlier, that the Patriots had fallen behind in a game. Brian had absolute confidence that Tom Brady and the offense would move the ball down the field again. He was also terribly nervous about the potential ramification of that scenario. Would the Patriots only make it far enough to try a field goal, meaning Brian would be required to throw the most pressure-packed and scrutinized snap of his life? Or would they be able to score a touchdown and thereby allow Brian to stay away from the drama he so desperately wanted to avoid? Brian prayed: *Please, God, let us score a touchdown so we don't have to kick a field goal. And then we can go for two so we don't even have to kick an extra point.*

Brian would never know whether it was actually God or just a bunch of teammates who answered his prayer. Either way, he was tremendously relieved when the offense completed an eleven-play, sixty-eight-yard drive by scoring a go-ahead touchdown (on a one-yard Brady pass to Mike Vrabel) with only 2:51 left on the clock. Ahead by five points, the Patriots indeed elected to go for a two-point conversion, and they were successful, on a Kevin Faulk run, which gave them a lead of 29–22. *Thank you, Lord.* With so little time remaining, Brian did not think it possible that the Panthers would again come back against the best defense in the NFL.

But he was wrong. What had started as a defensive slugfest had somehow escalated into a full-scale offensive shootout, and Carolina was by no means out of ammunition. The Panthers started on their own twenty. As they moved down the field, Brian kept telling himself: *This cannot be happening.* After seven plays, though, the Panthers were right where they wanted to be, back in the end zone, on a twelve-yard touchdown pass from Delhomme to wide receiver Ricky Proehl. The extra point was good, tying the score at 29–29. So much for all the predictions of a low-scoring and perhaps even dull game. This was already one of the most exciting Super Bowls in history—and it could very well be the first to stretch into overtime.

"Now the only question is have the Carolina Panthers left too much time on the clock for the New England Patriots?" analyst Daryl "Moose" Johnston said on the primary international telecast. "We're sitting here with 1:08 left to go in regulation time. Does Adam Vinatieri have a chance to redeem himself with a game-winning field goal in regulation?" Brian did not hear any of that on the sideline, of course, but he would have been hard-pressed to formulate a more terrifying collection of syllables. A field goal to win it in the final seconds? *Lord, no. Please, no. Anything but that.* With his friend and former teammate John Kasay preparing to kick off for Carolina, Brian would have given just about anything in the world to see a return all the way for a touchdown. If that were not to occur, he would be equally thrilled to see Brady make a heroic touchdown pass to win the game. Once they had the ball on offense, though, the Patriots probably would not be aggressive enough for that to happen, Brian thought. Much to his dismay, they would probably just try to get in position to win the game on a last-second field goal, meaning he would be mercilessly thrown into harm's way.

The chance of a game-winning kickoff return—slim as it was— quickly disappeared altogether due to a stunning mistake by Kasay. Trying to kick the ball into the right corner of the field, he instead hooked it out of bounds at about the eighteen-yard line. He would later say that when he ripped through the ball with his left foot, he caught it a little high and outside. It was only a matter of inches . . . but a monumental error. Although the bad kick eliminated any opportunity for the Patriots to score on a return, it also meant that they would start on offense with excellent field position, all the way out at their forty-yard line.

Field goal, Brian thought. *It's all coming down to a field goal. There's no way out of it.* Both his heart and mind were racing. He threw some practice snaps into a net on the sideline—pretending that each snap was the real thing and repeatedly reminding himself to relax and release to the target. If he had to go on the field, that was the one prevailing thought he wanted to have in his head: just relax and release to the target.

He paced. He prayed. *Please, Lord, if this is happening, please give me the strength I'm going to need.* He looked up and watched as Brady started moving the team forward. Two completions to Troy Brown put the Patriots at the Carolina forty-four-yard line. *Still a shot at a touchdown? Any chance at all?*

Only twenty seconds remained. Brady picked up four more yards on a pass to tight end Daniel Graham, then called for a time-out. With fourteen seconds left and the ball on the forty, the end zone was pretty much out of the question. The Patriots were definitely thinking field goal, and they had time for one more play to get within range for Vinatieri. Offensive coordinator Charlie Weis called for a play known in Patriots lingo as "Gun Trips Right 80 Rock OPEQ." In basic English, it meant that wide receivers Troy Brown and Deion Branch would run a combination route on the right side of the field, with Brown shallow and Branch running a deep out pattern toward the sideline. Depending on the defense, Brady could go to either guy. Taking the snap in shotgun formation, he quickly surveyed the defense and saw the Panthers go hard after the shallow route, meaning that Branch would probably break open farther down the field . . . and that was exactly the way it played out. Branch made his cut toward the sideline, Brady put the ball right where it needed to be, and the Patriots had a seventeen-yard gain to the Carolina twenty-three. With nine seconds left, they immediately called their final time-out.

It was time for the field-goal unit.

Brian was standing on the left side of the bench, opposite the end of the field into which the Patriots would be kicking. Ken Walter, already up by the sideline, turned and called to him, "Kinch,

Kinch, we're on the field." And out they went—along with Adam Vinatieri.

Forty-eight days earlier, Brian had been minding his own business with a collection of seventh graders in the comfortable seclusion of a small classroom in Louisiana. The next day, after his tryout with the Patriots, he had stood in the team cafeteria at Gillette Stadium and told Bill Belichick: "... whoever you choose will probably have the team's entire season in his hands at some point." Sure enough, that moment was about to come.

Nothing else mattered now. Not the thirteen years of professional football Brian had played before this whole remarkable odyssey with the Patriots. Not the hundreds of snaps he had thrown into pillows back at the hotel or the long I-want-out conversation with Scott Pioli. Not even his weak start in the first half or the invisible blanket of dread in which he had remained tightly wrapped—suffocatingly so—as the final minutes of the fourth quarter had ticked away. None of that mattered now because his entire career in athletics was about to be forever defined and branded, for good or for bad, by one upside-down, backward toss of a football. And no matter what the outcome, it would walk this world with Brian—more indelible than any tattoo—for the rest of his days.

Eighteen

Eight hundred miles away, Harper LeBel was at his home in Suwanee, Georgia, watching the game on television in his bedroom. He had never liked to attend Super Bowl parties because he preferred to concentrate on the game without the distractions of a social gathering. And this was exactly the kind of situation where he wanted to be totally locked in. After all, that guy running out on the field with Adam Vinatieri and Ken Walter could very well have been him. Seven weeks earlier, LeBel had been extremely disappointed when the Patriots did not select him to be their new long snapper after the tryout at which he had auditioned along with Brian and two others. Ever since then, he had been watching the Patriots to see how they would finish the season.

Now he had such mixed feelings: *Man, I wish that was me out there . . . so easily could have been. But what a great situation for Brian. Part of a last-second field goal to win the Super Bowl? What better scenario could you possibly make up? This is awesome. Perfect! It's what you dream about.*

Of course, LeBel had no way of knowing that while he was thinking of it as an ideally fashioned dream, Brian was just trying to survive what for him felt much more like a no-way-out nightmare.

Jogging onto the field, clinging to whatever hint of composure he had left, Brian told himself: *Just eliminate everything else—just block out everything else—and get it done.*

Walter and Vinatieri gave each other a fist bump.

"Let's do this," Walter said.

Mark Bavaro was watching with his wife, Susan, at their home in Boxford, Massachusetts. Having had that lunch with Brian two days before the Patriots left Boston for the Super Bowl, Bavaro knew better than almost anyone that the ball was about to be in the wrong guy's hands. Earlier in the game, after seeing Brian bounce snaps on both a punt and an extra point, Bavaro had concluded: "He's lost it. If this game comes down to a field goal, the Patriots are screwed. I cannot believe fate has taken this turn for this poor guy." And now? If Bavaro were forced to make a bet, his money would have to be on Brian blowing the snap. Bavaro could not bring himself to say the words out loud, but his overriding thought was: *Boy, you know, sometimes God is just cruel.* That was how bad he felt for Brian. Bavaro was still hoping that everything would somehow turn out okay for his friend. He was praying for Brian. But he also feared that the circumstances were simply overwhelming.

One thing was certain: the Panthers would be charging hard to try to get their second field-goal block of the day. Carolina special-teams coach Scott O'Brien had not changed his plan of attack since that block in the second quarter. The Panthers would again be loading up inside and trying to use the "A" gap between Brian and the left guard to create a point of entry and get a hand on the ball. Obviously, this was a must-rush situation for Carolina, with all eleven guys coming, and everyone knew that. The way O'Brien saw it, the outcome would be determined by the most basic element of football: execution. *Our execution versus theirs.*

Larry Izzo suddenly thought about the knife incident at breakfast. Standing on the sideline with fellow linebacker Ted Johnson, Izzo no longer thought it was so funny that the long snapper had done such a silly thing just hours before the game.

"Oh, no, Kinchen's hand!" Izzo said.

"Oh, geez," Johnson said.

And they left it at that.

The stadium sound system blared KC and the Sunshine Band's 1976 hit "(Shake, Shake, Shake) Shake Your Booty" during the time-out. As terrified as Brian was, it could have been playing Beethoven and he never would have known the difference. How rattled was he? When the Patriots' field-goal unit huddled up to prepare for action, Brian was supposed to stand directly across from Ken Walter, but he instead planted himself immediately to the left of the holder. "Kinch, get in the huddle," Walter told his friend.

On the Carolina sideline, thirteen-year NFL veteran John Kasay, one of the most reliable and admired players in Panthers history, stood with his arms folded across his chest, slowly shaking his head. He felt so responsible for the fact that the Patriots were about to line up for what might be the winning kick. It made no difference to him that the 2003 season would always be remembered as one of his best or that the Panthers might not even be in the Super Bowl without all that he had done with his left foot. So what if he had established a team record by making twenty-two consecutive field goals without a miss and had converted four game-winning kicks of his own? All he could think about was the out-of-bounds kick-off that had allowed the Patriots to start this drive on the forty-yard line and had greatly contributed to the position they were now in.

I cannot believe this, Kasay thought.

He had long followed a self-imposed rule for moments like this. Kasay would never allow himself to wish a bad kick on an opposing kicker because he knew exactly how it felt to miss one, and he certainly understood the consequences. He had seen a lot of people lose their jobs. No, he could never bring himself to wish ill on the opposing kicker, not even in the Super Bowl, not even when he wanted so desperately to somehow get back on the field and do something to atone for his costly kickoff. Arms crossed and head shaking, Kasay was entirely helpless. All he could do was watch and wait.

Brian did not bother moving to his assigned spot in the huddle, but it really made no difference. How could such a formality possibly matter now? With Brian by his side, Walter spoke in his usual role as play-caller for the field-goal team. "Guys, this is for the world championship," he said. "We've already had one blocked today. Do whatever you got to do. World champs! Field goal on Kinch." Instead of relying on the snap count of a quarterback, the way an offense would, the field-goal team would simply jump into action whenever Brian made his first movement, and those last words were to remind everyone of that. "Field goal on Kinch. Ready. Break!"

Approaching the line of scrimmage, Brian told himself: *I'll remember this moment for the rest of my life. This will define my career.* So much for being able to block out everything but his mantra of relaxing and releasing. Making things even worse, his mind then took an abrupt dive to a terribly negative pairing of images: He thought of Trey Junkin throwing the bad snap that cost the New York Giants a playoff game the year before. And he briefly contemplated the ugly, painful concept of throwing the ball over Walter's head. With so much at stake, such a blunder would be dramatically worse even than the Junkin fiasco that had generated so much media attention and had caused so much anguish for the man and his family.

Junkin and his wife, Sarah, were home in Winnfield, Louisiana, watching every moment of the Super Bowl coverage on CBS. Trey had heard that Brian was back in the NFL after having been out for a few years, but he had no idea that he'd been having such a difficult time. Before the game had even started, Trey and Sarah had talked about Brian, and Trey had told her, "He'll be fine as long as he doesn't think about what he's doing. That's what got me in trouble—too much thinking." Now that Brian was about to make the biggest snap of his life, Junkin returned to the same thought. In the silence of his mind, Junkin offered his advice to the man who was currently the loneliest long snapper on the planet: *Don't think about what you need to do with the ball. Just get in your stance and fire it back there the same way you have always done it.*

All eyes would soon be on the football now resting at the twenty-three-yard line. Before lowering himself over the ball, Brian slightly lifted his right leg and gently flexed it at the knee, then did the same with his left leg. An intentional last-second stretch? Or was it simply a matter of nerves having their way with him? Brian would never really know. He was in quite a fog by this point. Walter and Vinatieri had already picked out their spot in the turf at the thirty-one-yard line—the field-goal attempt would be a forty-one yarder from there—and the fingers of Walter's left hand were fixed on it so that Vinatieri could lock in on the target. The last thing Brian said to himself was: *Don't be tentative. You cannot be tentative.*

Brian positioned himself over the ball. He worked his hands to get a good grip on it. But then one of the game officials, umpire Jeff Rice, suddenly jumped in from behind the Carolina line to stop the whole thing. He was waving his arms over his head to signal a stoppage in play before it even started. The Panthers were taking a time-out of their own. It was nothing unusual for an opponent to try to ice a kicker and force him to think a little more at such a critical moment. What the Panthers could not have known, though, was that they had really been thinking about the wrong guy. The long snapper was the one who most felt like he was being put in a deep freeze.

On the Patriots' sideline, linebacker Don Davis went to his right knee, with his right hand leaning on his helmet, which rested on the ground beside him, and he did what came naturally for him. He put his head down and prayed. His words were directly related to everything he and Brian had talked about—and prayed about—earlier in the week after Brian had talked to Scott Pioli about wanting to leave the team. "Okay, God, this is the moment," Davis began. "This is why Brian went through all that. He's covered in prayer. Again, devil, you're a liar. Get away from him. God, let your glory be shown."

Walter took advantage of the time-out to let Brian know that he and Vinatieri had been in a bad spot the first time they had lined up. There was a depression in the ground right where they had set up behind Brian. "See if you can move the ball a little to the right," Walter said. "About six inches to the right and we'll be good."

On CBS, Greg Gumbel and Phil Simms spoke about Vinatieri and the extremely difficult job of a kicker at a time like this. "There just cannot be any more pressure on a football player," Simms said. Of course, he had no idea what was going on inside the helmet of the long snapper—that anonymous number forty-six of the Patriots.

When the second time-out finally came to an end and Brian got back over the ball, he made the slight adjustment to the right and once again gave himself final instructions: *Don't be tentative. Just throw it hard.* Other than his own words, Brian could not hear a thing.

All over Baton Rouge, Parkview students and their families were glued to televisions, waiting to see what would happen. No matter what the outcome, Brian's seventh graders would certainly have something out of the ordinary to talk about in school the next day.

Lori Kinchen was sitting in the lower deck of the stadium, section 104, row EE, seat 8. Actually, she was not really sitting so much as she was just all scrunched up in one big bundle of terribly frayed nerves. Lori felt ill, literally sick to her stomach. She knew that if Brian threw a bad snap and cost the Patriots the game, he would never be able to live it down, and the recurring thought of that actually made her feel like she was about to throw up. *What will Brian be like if something bad happens?* To Lori, this was no longer about winning or losing the Super Bowl. It was about the rest of her husband's life. It was about the whole future of her family. Austin, Hunter, and McKane had never seen their mom so distraught over a football game. (Logan was sitting elsewhere with other family members.) Tears rolled down Lori's cheeks. She leaned forward and buried her head in her hands. "I can't watch," she said. "I can't watch."

Walter and Vinatieri had a much better spot in the turf this time. Vinatieri kept his eyes on it as Walter put his right hand up in a fist toward the line of scrimmage. When Walter was ready for the ball, he would open his fist, flashing his hand to indicate that the release of the snap would then be up to Brian. Walter wanted so badly to feel the pebbled leather of that ball in his hands. He was convinced that no matter where Brian threw that thing, he was going to make the play and get the ball down for Vinatieri.

After only a slight pause, Walter flashed his hand. At long last, the moment of truth had arrived. Brian sent his arms back through his legs and unleashed the ball. He followed through with his hands all the way to his target. And Walter could tell from the instant he saw the ball coming: the snap was perfect! It was a tight spiral and directly in line with Walter's right shoulder—precisely how he wanted it thrown and where he liked to receive it. Walter snatched the ball out of the air as fast as he could, and even the laces were right where he wanted them, facing up, meaning that he could immediately make his placement without first having to turn the ball. Walter had plenty of time to place the ball exactly the way Vinatieri liked it, tilting slightly forward and to the right.

Vinatieri ripped through the ball with his right foot. And this time the ball went over the Carolina line with plenty of room to spare . . . appearing to be right on target as it continued climbing and advancing through the air.

"Looks good!" Greg Gumbel exclaimed on CBS.

Having done an excellent job of holding his position in the middle of the line, and of staying on his feet throughout the brief but hard-fought battle up front, Brian lifted his eyes and saw the ball going straight between the uprights with plenty of distance and without a moment of doubt. The kick was indeed good! For New England—both the team and the entire geographic region— the celebration was on.

Brian let loose with a primal scream that was unlike anything else that had ever come out of him. He jumped into the arms of offensive lineman Tom Ashworth, and they held each other in the glorious grip of victory. But wait! An alarming thought crossed Brian's mind: *Is it really over? Any flags on the ground?* He quickly surveyed the field. No penalty flags. *It's over! We did it!* With one perfect snap of a football, the snap of his life, Brian had gone from total anxiety and fear to absolute joy and jubilation. "Yes!" he shouted straight through the retractable but closed roof of that stadium and into the heavens. "Yes!"

As CBS showed a slow-motion replay of the game-winning field goal, Gumbel said, "Perfect spot by Walter. The perfect kick by Vinatieri." There was no mention whatsoever of Brian—just the way any self-respecting long snapper would have wanted the game to finish.

There was still the minor matter of four seconds remaining in the fourth quarter. But those final ticks of the clock only delayed the inevitable. New England easily shut down the ensuing kickoff return—with reserve linebacker Matt Chatham tackling ball carrier Rod Smart at the Carolina twenty-two-yard line—and Super Bowl XXXVIII was officially over. With a remarkable fifteenth victory in a row (only the 1972 Miami Dolphins had compiled a longer winning streak in a single season), the Patriots were 2003 champions of the National Football League. Players, coaches, and staff stormed the field, jumping, hugging, and shouting with both relief and euphoria. Huge confetti-blowing machines filled the air with the red, white, blue, and silver of the Patriots. Brian had never before been so thrilled—and so thankful—on a field of play. "Just purely elated," he would later recall, "like a young child getting a dream gift or something."

Nineteen

A portable stage was positioned at the center of the field for the presentation of the Vince Lombardi Trophy that goes to the winner of the Super Bowl. Team owner Robert Kraft, together with Bill Belichick, Scott Pioli, and a few players who starred in the game, would climb onto the platform for the presentation by NFL commissioner Paul Tagliabue and brief interviews by Jim Nantz of CBS. The rest of the New England staff and players would watch from the field.

Brian wanted his wife and children with him to share in the celebration, so he turned away to find them. He walked toward the stands on the Patriots' side of the field, targeting the general vicinity where Lori and the boys had been sitting, and he looked up through the still-falling confetti. Peering through the face mask of his helmet, which he had not yet bothered to remove from his head, Brian was at first unable to pick his family out of the crowd. He threw up his arms in frustration, but then he found them, and he hurried over to the wall that separated the stands from the area behind the New England bench. A friendly fan helped the Kinchen boys over the wall and passed them down to Brian, one at a time, from youngest to oldest. As Brian gathered in fourteen-year-old Austin, he saw tears of joy rolling down the cheeks of his first child, glistening, as were the braces in his mouth. Austin was at once crying and smiling. He was old enough to know how long and hard his father had worked at the game of football, he was fully aware how much that last snap had to mean to his dad, and he was clearly overwhelmed by the sheer drama of it all. He was so happy and excited that he was simply incapable of controlling his emotions. It was one of the sweetest things Brian had ever seen. Right then, as if on cue, the Queen song "We Are the Champions" started playing over the stadium sound system:

I've paid my dues.

Time after time.

Once all the boys were settled on the field, Lori was the last Kinchen over the wall and into Brian's arms, literally hanging on him, arms draped over his shoulders—actually over his shoulder pads and jersey—and she, too, was crying. Brian held her in a tight embrace, his face mask banging against the right side of her face and bruising it, but what was a little physical discomfort at a time when she was practically numb with emotional overload?

"I can't believe it," Brian said.

"I know," Lori said. "Neither can I. I can't believe it."

Freddie Mercury of Queen was in full throat now:

No time for losers.

'Cause we are the champions . . . of the world!

Brian lowered Lori and stood her on the ground. He cradled McKane in his left arm. And off went the whole family—off to the middle of the field for an up-close view of the trophy ceremony.

The Kinchens worked their way through a throng of media types, lots of men and women carrying cameras and notebooks, and settled a few feet from the right side of the presentation platform. While Kraft held the Lombardi Trophy and made his acceptance remarks, Brian failed to maintain even a hint of decorum.

"Hey, Pioli," he shouted up at the podium, trying to get the attention of the man who four days earlier had persuaded him to stay with the team. "Scott . . . Scott . . . Scott!" Pioli finally located the source of the shouting and looked at his longtime friend. "You were right," Brian said. "You were right." Pioli smiled, and he saw tremendous emotion filling Brian's face, reading his expression as equal parts bliss and disbelief. Pioli figured that Brian was probably still working through something of a reality check: *Is all of this actually happening? Was I really part of the winning play in the Super Bowl?*

Belichick was next to take the trophy and speak with Jim Nantz. Then came Tom Brady, MVP of the game and now the youngest quarterback to win two NFL championships; and Adam Vinatieri, the first kicker to make game-winning field goals in the final seconds of two different Super Bowls. Nantz had already declared that what had just taken place was "the greatest Super Bowl game in history." Other football enthusiasts might debate that. If not the greatest, however, it was indisputably one of the most explosive and most exciting of all Super Bowls. After hearing countless predictions of a defensive struggle, New England and Carolina had produced eye-popping numbers on offense. The teams had combined for the second-most net yards (868) in Super Bowl history and in the final fifteen minutes had lit up the scoreboard with the most points (37) ever posted in any quarter of a Super Bowl.

While Nantz and Vinatieri talked about the overall drama of the game, though, Brian remained stuck on the singular challenge and personal triumph of that final snap. With Belichick still on the presentation platform, Brian yelled out to him several times before finally getting his attention. "Hey, Bill, did I get it done?" Brian shouted. Belichick responded with a quick thumbs-up before turning back to the onstage festivities.

Soon thereafter, Brian exchanged congratulations with Larry Izzo, the special-teams captain who had been sitting next to him at breakfast. "With the lacerated finger and everything, you got it done, my man," Izzo said. "I'm happy for you." Pointing to Brian's wounded hand, Izzo smiled and finished by saying, "Yeah, that's legendary now."

The on-field frolicking continued for a good while after the CBS interviews were done, and the Lombardi Trophy remained a primary focal point. Players passed it around, posed with it for pictures, and generally treated it as if it were the Hope diamond. While waiting his turn, Brian removed his jersey and shoulder pads, and he said, "Last time I'm taking these off. Ever. Done. The era's over." He happily put on an official championship T-shirt and cap.

When someone finally passed the trophy to Brian, he did not only hold it and stare at it. He also kissed it. Then he laughed at himself for putting his lips to the hardware. "I always thought that's so stupid when people do that," he said. But now it was his turn to act a fool. "Yeah, baby!" Brian shouted. "Whooo!" And then he went right back to laughing.

Once most of the fans had left the stadium and a majority of the players had cleared the field, Gus and Toni Kinchen were able to talk their way past security and down from the stands to see their son. Brian told his parents he was so exhausted—so emotionally spent—that he could hardly even stand.

Trying to put the intensity of the struggle against Carolina in perspective, New England linebacker Mike Vrabel would later make a comparison to one of the most celebrated boxing rivalries in history: "It was like Ali–Frazier out there. That's how it felt. We hit them, they hit us, we hit them, they hit us." Brian had a much grander scale of fighting on his mind. While embracing his dad, he told him that he had battled his way through the game feeling like Gideon, the Old Testament character who led a dramatically outnumbered army of three hundred men to save Israel from the Midianites. Gideon initially felt powerless against such overwhelming odds, but he ultimately conquered his opponent the same way Brian had just gone from feeling helpless to being victorious: by trusting in the providence of God.

After posing for one last picture on the field—this one with his mother and father in it—Brian looked around and realized that almost all of his teammates had gone inside to continue celebrating in the locker room. "Hey, I'm like the last one out here," he said. "I think I need to go." Brian could not take Lori with him. They would later meet up back at the team hotel. But he was not going anywhere without his boys. Brian rounded up Austin, Hunter, Logan (now wearing his dad's oversize shoulder pads atop his eight-year-old frame), and McKane, and they all walked off the field together: a profoundly relieved and thankful man in his final exit as a professional athlete, and four boys who were just happy to be hanging out with their dad.

Walking with his sons through a hallway leading to the main area of the New England locker room, Brian glanced in the open door of a small room to his right, and he saw Bill Belichick's wife, Debby, visiting with a few other Patriots insiders. When he entered the room to say hello, Debby immediately went to hug him, and she also wasted no time before delivering a friendly jab.

"I'm barely speaking to you," Debby said. "But thank *God* you came through in the end!"

"I know," Brian said.

"Congratulations!"

"I know I put Bill through hell all week."

"That's all right," she said.

There was more celebratory hugging and hollering in the locker room. Then Brian went to the training room to have someone unwrap his finger and take a look. Team physician Bert Zarins put three stitches in it. Brian then showered, dressed, and gathered up his belongings, even pulling down the nameplate from above his locker and handing it to Austin for safe keeping. (It would eventually be added to the already overflowing collection of football memorabilia in Brian's home office.)

On his way out of the locker room, Brian happened to cross paths with Bill Belichick. They hugged. Then Brian offered an apology: "Sorry about all I put you through the last couple weeks."

"Oh, that's fine, Brian," Belichick said. "It doesn't matter. We won. A win is a win." Brian chuckled at that last statement—a win is a win—because it was such an overused Belichick classic. But it had never before meant as much to Brian as it did now.

"Thanks for having me," he told his coach. "Thanks for letting me be a part of all this."

Brian took his sons with him on a team bus from the stadium back to the hotel, and they sat in the back row so they could all stretch out together. After a while, having been distracted on his cell phone for a few minutes, Brian noticed that four-year-old McKane had wandered off, not that he could have gone all that far. "Where's McKane?" Brian asked the other boys, but none of them knew, so Dad went up the aisle looking for him.

Brian was surprised, and also somewhat embarrassed, when he discovered where his son had ended up. In an aisle seat on the right side of the bus, McKane was sitting in Tom Brady's lap, chatting away as if the two of them, one on a weekend getaway from his pre-kindergarten class, the other freshly crowned as MVP of the Super Bowl, were old buddies. McKane did not even know what his seatmate—looking all GQ in his suit and tie and stubble—did for a living. He was simply a random guy on the bus who was nice enough to spend some time with him. Brian apologized to Brady for McKane's intrusion. But Brady assured his teammate that he had enjoyed the visit.

"Your kid is awesome, so cute," he said. "And now I know your home phone number, street address, city, and state." McKane's teacher had required him to learn all of that for class, and now it was apparently some of his best material for conversation with an adult. Brian laughed and shook his head. "Everyman" at the Super Bowl had yet another memory to pack away for the rest of his life: the image of his youngest child doing some serious post-game bonding—well, okay, basically just killing time on a bus—with one of the most famous athletes in all of professional sports.

After the team party in a hotel ballroom, at which everyone was treated to musical performances by Kid Rock and Aerosmith, Lori was too tired to stay awake. But Brian had caught a second wind and was still too wired from all the drama of the game to even think about sleeping, so he turned on the television. He did not count the number of times he watched the same Super Bowl highlights being replayed on ESPN throughout the wee hours of the morning. But no matter how many times he saw the same clips—including footage of the winning field goal—he never stopped enjoying them.

With so many thoughts about the game and its aftermath going round and round in his head, Brian decided to spend some time with his tape recorder. At 5:15 in the morning, he pushed the record button and started talking about the day he finally earned a title that nobody could ever take away from him: Super Bowl champion.

He spoke about his terrible pre-game warm-up and about his weak start in the first half. He spoke about the unbelievable tension of the fourth quarter and about everything that went into the final snap of his career. And then—in no particular order—he filled his tape with a variety of details from during and after the game. As many topics as Brian covered, there were two primary thoughts that stood out as headlines above everything else:

One, Brian was thrilled beyond description with the way his career had ultimately come to a close. Granted, his overall performance with the Patriots had been far from stellar, and his loss of confidence had taken him to the brink of disaster. But how could he possibly ask for a better ending than having his hands on the ball for the winning play in the Super Bowl? "I couldn't be happier," Brian said into the tape recorder.

Two, he finally thought he understood why he had gone through such a horrible couple of weeks leading up to that final snap. By being deprived of his usual confidence—"I was at the end of my rope," Brian said—he was left in a position in which all he could do was rely on his faith. "I knew that I could not accomplish what I had to do without God," he said. "It was like he was just stripping me down to where I had to just depend on him, and I did, because I had no clue where that ball was going to go."

Twenty

Two days after the Super Bowl, Boston threw a victory parade for the Patriots, with an estimated million and a half people lining the streets from Copley Square to City Hall Plaza. Fans cheered and screamed with affection. They waved banners and signs. Confetti rained down from the windows of office buildings. Brian had never seen anything like it—so many people so animated about the outcome of a football game. At the end of the parade route, Bill Belichick and a few players offered brief remarks to the crowd. There was a lot more cheering and screaming. Then the massive gathering started to break up. After posing for a final photo with the Lombardi Trophy and saying good-bye to his teammates, Brian was officially done as a New England Patriot—and as a professional football player. This time, he had perfect closure. He went straight to Logan Airport and flew home to Baton Rouge.

The next day, Wednesday, February 4, 2004, Brian was back at Parkview Baptist Middle School. Three days after snapping the football on the winning play in the Super Bowl, he was again a seventh-grade teacher. But his first day back was far from routine. Local television crews showed up for interviews. Brian spoke in a school assembly about his time with the Patriots. He received hugs and handshakes all morning—from students and teachers alike—and several students asked for his autograph. A few of his fellow teachers teased him good-naturedly about being such a "big celebrity" now that he was a Super Bowl champion.

"Yeah, right," Brian responded with a smile. "Give it about two days, and everything will be right back to normal."

He was wrong about that. Although everything at school would indeed settle down by the end of the week—with Brian getting to know his new students and enjoying the transition back into teaching—the afterglow of victory would continue to shine brightly beyond the walls of Parkview. There is no such thing as a victory lap in football. For Brian, however, life after the Super Bowl sure started to feel like one—or maybe it would be more accurate to call it a victory *tour*. There was no overall structure or planning involved. It was just a matter of all the excitement leading to one special event after another.

Two of the most significant occasions—visiting the White House in May, and getting his Super Bowl ring in June—came within the context of team tributes. Most of what Brian experienced, though, he was invited to do as an individual. It was nothing unusual for someone who had just played in a Super Bowl to receive a generous amount of attention, especially when he happened to live in a football-loving state such as Louisiana. But the unique nature of Brian's story—from Bible class to the Super Bowl—greatly elevated the level of interest. So what if he had played the most obscure position on the field? He was a world champion! That was all anyone cared about, and it opened many doors.

The Krewe of Jupiter placed him on a float as master of ceremonies for its Mardi Gras parade through the streets of Baton Rouge. The mayor of Lake Charles honored him with a key to the city. The Louisiana State Penitentiary at Angola invited him behind bars to encourage prisoners who excelled in its recreation program. The Capital Area United Way gave him the honorary title "community champion" and asked for his help in its annual fund-raising campaign. Brian had never before received so many requests for appearances and speaking engagements. Schools, churches, youth groups, civic organizations, local companies—they all wanted Brian to join them for some sort of event.

The beauty of his story was that it had something for everyone. Although it was the powerful platform of sports that gave him a voice as well as an audience, Brian used that platform to deliver a universal and inspirational message of hope that extended far beyond the sphere of athletics. His was a story about second chances and the empowering notion that virtually anything is possible. It was about the importance of family and relationships. Ultimately, the story of Brian Kinchen was all about faith and the glory of God.

The response to his presentation was invariably positive—and Brian cherished the thought that he might be touching the lives of others. Schedule permitting, he never turned down an invitation to speak about his Super Bowl experience.

Brian finally got the retirement party he had long wanted but never really felt comfortable about having. Not until now—now that he was absolutely certain that his playing days were done. Close to a hundred people attended his party at the LSU football facility. The guests enjoyed the unique decorations: a colorful display of helmets and game jerseys from each of the five NFL teams for which Brian had played. A highlight video offered glimpses of Brian playing tight end and scoring touchdowns in collegiate and NFL games long gone. Family, friends, and former teammates took turns sharing lighthearted jabs and poignant memories. The most intriguing statement of the evening came from the honoree himself. "The success-oriented part of my life is over," Brian said. "Now it's time to move on to significance."

A longtime family friend, Craig Greene, stopped by the Kinchens' home one day because he happened to be in town and had something he wanted to show Brian and Lori: his videotape from the Super Bowl. Greene was a Baton Rouge native now living in Houston, where he was an orthopedic surgeon in residency. He had gone to the Super Bowl with Brian's brother Todd and had shot the video from their seats in the upper deck of Reliant Stadium. Brian and Lori had already seen the CBS broadcast of the game on tape. But Greene's footage was much more personal. He had shots of Brian warming up before the game and standing on the field near Beyoncé Knowles as she sang the national anthem. He had dramatic shots of Brian before, during, and after the game-winning field goal. There was even tape of the four Kinchen boys and Lori being passed down from the stands to Brian for the post-game celebration on the field.

Glancing at Brian as he processed those images for the first time, Greene had no doubt that his friend was totally locked in. *Like a bride watching her wedding video,* he thought. Brian was indeed consumed by what he was seeing. It felt wonderful to relive all those remarkable moments without having to worry about a bad snap or the overall outcome of the game. Yet he also could not pretend away a jarring thought.

"Can you imagine if I had messed up that snap and we lost?" Brian said.

"Oh, my God," Lori said. "I can't even think about that."

On Sunday, June 13, 2004, Brian and Lori flew from Pittsburgh—where Brian had just played in hockey star Mario Lemieux's celebrity golf tournament—to Boston. The Kinchens had one final date with the Patriots: a celebratory dinner and the "Ceremony of Rings" at the Chestnut Hill home of team owner Robert Kraft. For professional athletes, a championship ring was the utmost measure of a job well done—the quintessential symbol of success. Rings had become such a focal point for athletes that many would not even use the words "winning a championship" when discussing their ultimate goal. "Getting a ring"—that was the phrase that said it all in the lexicon of sports.

Brian already had one championship ring from the 2003 season sitting at home—an impressive token of appreciation for his volunteer coaching with Nick Saban and the LSU Tigers. That made him the answer to a trivia question: he would forever be the guy who won both a college championship ring and a Super Bowl ring in the same season. Brian was not thinking about anything like that. He just wanted to see his ring from the Patriots. He wanted to feel it on his hand.

Brian and Lori were late for dinner. Traveling from the golf tournament, they could not do anything about that. At least they arrived before the unveiling of the rings. The Kinchens were seated in time to hear Belichick and Kraft speak about the splendor of the season and the significance of the rings. Then each player was given a cherrywood box. Brian opened the box containing his size 13½ ring, and he could hardly believe what he was seeing. It was not only that a Super Bowl ring had actually been personalized with his name and his number forty-six. He was also stunned by the sheer size and gaudiness of it. Cast in white gold, the ring was adorned with 104 diamonds—5.05 carats in all—and weighed 3.8 ounces. No NFL franchise had ever designed a heavier Super Bowl ring. Brian loved the overall look of it and the way it told a story by incorporating elements such as the Lombardi Trophy, Gillette Stadium, the Patriots logo, and the fifteen-game winning streak that ended the season (represented by fifteen full-cut diamonds on top of the bezel). He especially enjoyed seeing the word "WORLD" screaming out from one side of the crest and "CHAMPIONS" from the other. *It's like a piece of art,* Brian thought. He was also impressed by its appraised value of twenty thousand dollars. Still, nobody would have faulted him for wondering this: was he really looking at a ring, or had someone mistakenly placed a hood ornament in his box?

Brian held out the ring for Lori to see. He handed it to her. But she gave it right back to him.

"Put it on," she said.

He did—and it was a perfect fit.

For a man who had always believed that performance was the only path to affirmation, that mammoth hunk of precious metal and stones was a sight to behold as he stared down at his right hand. Sixteen years after being picked in the last round of the NFL draft—three years after feeling painfully empty because he thought his football career was done and gone—Brian now owned sparkling evidence of the only thing he had ever really wanted from the game he loved, had ever thought he needed from it. Validation.

Brian quickly learned that the ring was a magnet. A boy who wanted his autograph on the flight back to Louisiana certainly would not have known he was a football player without the youngster's eyes first being drawn to the most conspicuous piece of jewelry on the plane. While Brian and Lori waited for their luggage in the New Orleans airport, a middle-aged man approached Brian, pointed to the ring, and asked if he played for the Saints. Clearly, the man did not know much about the local team. The woeful Saints had played thirty-seven NFL seasons without ever making it to a Super Bowl.

"Uh, no, I don't play for the Saints," Brian said. "I played for the New England Patriots."

"Oh," the man said. "Well, congratulations."

Before Brian even got home, he knew he would wear the ring only for special occasions. It was simply too bulky and awkward for everyday wear; he told Lori that maybe each player should also get a "baby" replica that would be easier to carry around on his hand. Plus, the ring made him uncomfortable because of the way it drew attention, as if he were asking for people to gawk at him and connect the dots to his status as a Super Bowl champion. His first thought was to keep the ring packed away, in its wooden display box, on a shelf in his home office. He kept all his other football memorabilia in the office. But Brian also thought of something else: the way so many people had been asking him, even before he got his ring, if they could see it. So he decided to keep the ring somewhere he would always have easy access to it—in his car. Brian slipped his newest piece of jewelry into a small cloth bag intended to protect a pair of sunglasses, and he put the bag in the console of his Toyota Sequoia.

For months, the ring went in and out of that vehicle. It was always a major hit when Brian went somewhere to speak. People wanted to see it up close and maybe even get to try it on. Depending on the size and nature of his audience, Brian sometimes passed the ring around the room, inevitably leading to a chorus of oohs and aahs. Then there were the more personal moments with friends and acquaintances who had followed his run to the Super Bowl— or had at least heard about it—and now wanted to check out the symbolic keepsake that came with being a champion. Those were the moments that meant the most to Brian. He was sometimes embarrassed by the way people would go overboard with their excitement and praise, but he also felt so good about others being able to enjoy what had happened to him.

Friends and family noticed something interesting as Brian continued to share his football story with others. He also started sharing more of himself. He seemed to be more relaxed than usual, more content, and he intentionally made more of an effort to keep in touch with friends. The people closest to him did not know exactly how to define what they were seeing. A mellowing? A new comfort level? A newfound sense of peace?

Over time, Brian identified a paradox that came with his long-desired validation as a professional athlete: finally getting it made him realize it was something he had never really needed in the first place. Ultimately, the true value of that ring was the way it provided a platform to reach others and impact their lives. There was no identifiable epiphany, no single moment when Brian felt a proverbial lightbulb flashing on for him to understand this. Rather, it was a slow, gradual process that brought clarity. Brian just knew that every time he had a speaking engagement, every time he had the opportunity to inspire others by sharing what God had done in his life, he felt a greater sense of purpose—a greater sense of the "significance" he had talked about at his retirement party—than he had ever experienced on any field of play. With that in mind, he came to view his ring more as a means than an end.

A friend had once told Brian about a favorite line from a movie called *Cool Runnings,* which is loosely based on the story of the 1988 Jamaican Olympic bobsled team. On the eve of the climactic race, the coach, played by John Candy, has a heart-to-heart talk with the team's driver, during which he tells him, "A gold medal is a wonderful thing. But if you're not enough without it, you'll never be enough with it." That was exactly how Brian came to feel about his Super Bowl ring. He would always look back on his experience with the Patriots as the realization of a dream. He would always be deeply grateful for the way everything had turned out. But having that ring did not make him any more complete than he had ever been. It contributed nothing to making him the man he had always wanted to be—a man who put God and family above all else.

Brian started using that movie line in his speeches: *If you're not enough without it, you'll never be enough with it.* The way he saw and presented that statement, it was not only about a gold medal or a championship ring. It had a universal meaning that spoke to so many things people choose to chase in this world—money, fancy cars, big houses, lofty job titles. Brian spelled out for his audiences why he was exactly the same person with or without any ring on his finger: "Because God looks at me the same . . . and because I know who I am in the eyes of my creator. If I don't seek my significance and love from God—the only true source of it—then all the rest is just a veiled attempt to fill a void that only he can fill."

For people who shared Brian's spiritual beliefs, those words were a perfect conclusion to a story they would view as "testimony"—his public profession of a religious experience and the deep faith that guided him. That was certainly the way his students at Parkview would see it. Yet the underlying lesson applied equally well in a secular setting: If you want to be a person of significance and love, you do not need to seek and obtain the same things so many others are chasing and collecting. You never need to *have* enough. You need only to look within yourself to figure out whether you *are* enough.

Brian could have incorporated the closing lines from that *Cool Runnings* scene into his standard presentation.

Bobsled driver: "Hey, Coach, how will I know if I'm enough?"
Coach: "When you cross that finish line, you'll know."

Brian knew exactly what he would someday be looking for at his own finish line. He would be looking to see what had become of the "living legacy" he wrote about in the back of his Bible one lonely night in New England. He would be taking measure of himself based on what had become of his four sons.

Acknowledgments

Right from the start, I warned Brian Kinchen about what goes into the making of a book. I told him: if I'm going to write this story, I'll need more of your time than you could possibly imagine. Brian gave me all the time I needed, and that was only the beginning of his gifts. He also gave me his trust. He shared his family and friends with me. He opened his home and office to me. I thank Brian and his wonderful wife, Lori, for showing me nothing but kindness and cooperation as I scribbled the best I could and kept returning with more questions. Other Kinchens were equally welcoming: Brian's parents, Gus and Toni; his brothers, Cal and Todd; and his sons, Austin, Hunter, Logan, and McKane.

Research was by no means limited to one family, though. I interviewed more than a hundred people for this book, and I am enormously grateful for the input of all who participated. I'd like to thank those who helped most by listing their names.

From the 2003 New England Patriots: Matt Chatham, Don Davis, Christian Fauria, Damon Huard, Larry Izzo, Scott Pioli, Anthony Pleasant, and Ken Walter.

From around the National Football League: Ernie Accorsi, Mark Bavaro, Bill Curry, Al Del Greco, Tom Goode, Trey Junkin, John Kasay, Harper LeBel, Ted Marchibroda, Scott Nicolas, Scott O'Brien, Dan O'Leary, Chance Pearce, Dave Shula, Don Shula, Jan Stenerud, Matt Stover, Vinny Testaverde, and Mike Westhoff.

From Louisiana State University (LSU): Chris Carrier, Steve Damen, Paul Dietzel, Tommy Hodson, Donnie Jones, Terry Lewis, Gant Petty, Don "Scooter" Purvis, Warren Rabb, Ruffin Rodrigue, Nick Saban, Jerry Stovall, Jerry Sullivan, and Ed Zaunbrecher.

From Parkview Baptist School: Dairon Bueche, Jennie Garland, Wesley Perkins, Cooper Pope, Sonya Pruitt, and Ashley Thornton.

From elsewhere in Louisiana: Odom Graves, Craig Greene, Darryl Hamilton, Gordon McKernan, and Jeff Wampold.

Many others helped in a variety of ways.

Amy Brittain was reliable and efficient as a research assistant. I also want to thank the following professionals who took time to track down information and secure footage for me: Armen Keteyian of CBS, Jon Kramer and Josh Krulewitz of ESPN, and Ray Didinger and Ken Rodgers of NFL Films.

People in the LSU athletics department were—as I have always found them to be—extremely kind and accommodating. Big thanks go to Michael Bonnette, Wanda Carrier, Kent Lowe, Bill Martin, and Herb Vincent.

In addition to all the help I got that was directly related to gathering material for this book, I have also received immeasurable support in a number of other areas.

Cindy DiTiberio of HarperOne has exhibited tremendous faith in me. She has treated this project with great care and respect. Cindy, I thank you for being both a wonderful representative of your company and a woman of grace and integrity.

Tom Connolly is not only one of the best lawyers in America. He is also one of the best friends anyone could have. Others at the law firm of Harris, Wiltshire & Grannis—most notably Rob Carter— have also represented me exceptionally well. TC and Rob, please know how much I appreciate all your efforts.

Carl Cannon has been editing my work for twenty years. It is difficult to imagine a crueler fate. Yet he has somehow managed to red-ink his way through all five of my books. Carl, thank you, as always, for trying to salvage the pile of pages I gave to you. We made it through another one!

John Carroll is never second to anyone when it comes to influence on my career. He was my first newspaper editor and has been both mentor and friend throughout the whole of my adult life. In this case, though, he did come second, reading the manuscript and offering suggestions after Carl and I were done. John, thank you, as always, for caring about me and my work.

Friends and family were more than patient with me when I locked myself away to write. I thank the following for being so supportive and understanding: Al Adamsen, Dale Brown, Mark Brunell, David Ellington, Rusty Gorman, Jason Harper, Randy Hearon, Lauren Hochman, Bert Jones, Greg Katz, Daniella Landau, Carl Lewis, Mitch Loveman, Jim Marx, Peggy Marx, Richard Marx, Lisa Lynne Mathis, Eric Mogentale, Kim and Bonnie Nuxhall, Mike and Beth O'Shea, LJ and Carolyn and all the Oncales, Peter Ripka, Mark Schamel,

Dane Strother, Bret and Lori Talbot, Merv Wampold, and Mike Woodrow.

That brings me to the two people with whom I most closely share my days: my awesome wife, Leslie ("Po" to me); and my remarkable stepdaughter, Alex. I have yet to figure out how they put up with me while I'm working on a book, but I'm mighty fortunate that they do. Po and Alex, thank you for being here whenever I needed you most, for allowing me to go on and on with my endless stream of book talk, for giving me the time and space to do what I do.

Reading and Discussion Guide for
THE LONG SNAPPER

1. Brian lived a dream by playing thirteen years in the NFL, yet often looked at his career as a failure. Why do you think it's sometimes easy to allow disappointments to overshadow blessings?

2. As Brian contemplated whether or not to accept the tryout offer, he mentally processed a string of rejections that dotted his NFL career. Why do you think that caused him to second guess his decision? What are some rejections you've dealt with in your life? Have those rejections caused you to push forward or pull back?

3. Prior to 2003, Brian had never experienced a college or professional championship. In some ways, he had spent much of his career living up to his own expectations to follow in his father's footsteps (who had won a national

title at LSU). Have you ever had a similar need for validation?

4. Brian says that his return to the NFL wasn't about the money. It was about the opportunity to walk away from football on his own terms; in other words, he was playing with purpose. Can you think of a time when you were working strictly for the paycheck? Can you think of a time when you were motivated by a greater goal or purpose? How were the two situations different?

5. For much of his life, Brian sought approval through achievement. He would later credit growing up as a middle child for his self-diagnosed addiction to praise and recognition. In what ways do you usually seek approval? How important is the approval of others to you? Why do you think that's the case?

6. When Brian was dealing with some adversity, his father Gus wrote him an encouraging poem titled "Focus." Do you ever struggle with focus? How much of a difference does focus, or the lack thereof, have on your ability to reach goals? In what area of your life could you use more focus and a stronger work ethic?

7. Brian made sacrifices to fulfill his dream. He was away from family. He missed his son's birthday. He didn't get to help LSU—his alma mater for which he'd been volunteering during the season—prepare for the National Championship Game. What are some things you've

sacrificed for a personal goal? Was the end result worth the sacrifice?

8. Brian's return to the NFL wasn't as glamorous as people might think. In fact, it was full of mundane realities that many might consider downright boring. What are some things that might attract people to the kind of lifestyle Brian enjoyed for thirteen years? Do any of those things appeal to you? In general, why do people crave success? How important is material wealth and status to you?

9. Whether it was during practice or on game day, Brian found solace in his routine, and it helped him quickly readjust to the NFL mentality. To maintain a consistent regiment, it takes a good measure of discipline. How important is routine in your daily life? What happens when you break from that routine?

10. Anonymity is golden for the long snapper. As Brian has seen with other long snappers, the only time people talk about you is when you make a costly mistake. What are some real-world parallels to the precarious nature of Brian's old job? What are some responsibilities in your life that only get noticed when you mess them up? What role does consistency play when you approach those tasks?

11. From his hotel room in Foxboro, Brian watched LSU defeat Oklahoma for the national title. He especially enjoyed seeing reserve long snapper Gant Petty, an athlete he had been mentoring, do well in place of the suspended

starter. Have you ever mentored someone? Can you relate to Brian's feeling of fulfillment that came with his "student's" success?

12. One of the more touching letters Brian received was from a girl named Jennie Garland who thanked him for the impact he'd made on her life. Jennie's thoughtful note caught Brian off guard and reminded him of his important role as a teacher. Can you recall a time when you received unexpected fulfillment from something you do on a regular basis? What are some ways that you can impact others in your sphere of influence?

13. What is your personal definition of the world "purpose"? Brian had been measuring his self-worth based on performance. Have you ever lived that way? Did it help you achieve a satisfactory result?

14. Do you think it's important to have a written record of what you believe to be your purpose in life? What are some key points that might be found in your "life purpose statement"? What steps do you need to take in order to begin living out that statement?

15. Brian "had long felt that being a dad…was his greatest purpose in the world." Being away from family for an extended period of time caused him to realize the depth of that belief. This held especially true when he had to tell his son Logan that he wouldn't be home in time for his birthday. Have you ever felt like you were sacrificing your family for a personal goal? How do you find balance

between your role in the family (e.g., spouse, parent, child) and your need to fulfill a purpose?

16. On the surface, Brian seemed fine. Only a select few people knew there was anything wrong with his psyche. Covering up internal issues is a common practice. Are there any problems you're dealing with that no one else knows about? Why have you found it difficult to share them with others?

17. After Viniatieri's successful kick, the winning field goal was played over and over again. The broadcasters mentioned the perfect hold and the perfect kick, but there was no mention of the perfect snap. Strangely, Brian was hoping he wouldn't be mentioned during the game at all since long snappers are usually only highlighted for their mistakes. What are some good things you've done but never received credit or attention? Did it bother you that no one recognized your contribution?

18. At the end of the day, Brian could unequivocally say that the Super Bowl victory was worth the struggle. His risk in leaving the comforts of home and facing the potential for failure was not as great as the reward. Can you think of a time when your hard work and effort paid off in a big way? What are some risks you took in order to fulfill a dream?

19. Brian came to the realization that his desire for success had been quenched and now he was more interested in obtaining significance. What do you think is the difference

between success and significance? Do you feel like you've achieved either in your lifetime? Which is more personally fulfilling? Which do you think will be longer lasting?

20. As Brian became further removed from the Super Bowl victory, he realized more and more that the achievement could never fulfill him like his faith in God and his relationship with his family and friends. The big win and its spoils served "more as a means than an end." Have you ever found yourself searching for the next success in your life? Why do you think personal milestones never seem to be enough?

JEFFREY MARX is the *New York Times* bestselling author of *Season of Life* and recipient of the 1986 Pulitzer Prize for investigative reporting. He has also written for numerous publications including *Sports Illustrated, Newsweek, Time, The Washington Post,* the *Los Angeles Times* and *The Baltimore Sun.* Marx lives in Baton Rouge, Louisiana. Visit the author online at www.seasonoflife.com and www.jeffreymarx.org.

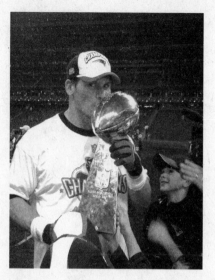

BRIAN KINCHEN is in his second year as the head football coach at Ascension Christian High School in Gonzales, Louisiana. He travels in the spring speaking about his faith journey as described in *The Long Snapper*. His two oldest sons, Austin and Hunter, are both playing football for LSU.